Monograph Supplements to the
Scottish Journal of Theology

General Editors

T. F. TORRANCE and J. K. S. REID

THE DOCTRINE OF THE TRINITY

IN THIS SERIES

THE DOCTRINE
OF THE TRINITY

GOD'S BEING IS IN BECOMING

━━●━━ ━━●━━ ━●━

EBERHARD JÜNGEL

LIBRARY ST. MARY'S COLLEGE
WILLIAM B. EERDMANS PUBLISHING COMPANY
Grand Rapids, Michigan

Published in the U.S.A. 1976 by
William B. Eerdmans Publishing Co.,
Grand Rapids, Michigan

First published 1976

© 1976 Translation. Scottish Academic Press Ltd.

Library of Congress Cataloging in Publication Data

Jüngel, Eberhard.
    The Doctrine of the Trinity.
    Translation of Gottes Sein ist im Werden.
    Includes bibliographical references and index.
    1. God—History of doctrines—20th century. 2. Barth, Karl,
1886–1968. I. Title.
BT101.B2718J813   231   76–20794
    ISBN 0–8028–3490–6

(rohmp) ᒐᒐ-ᑐᑕ-ᑲ ᑰᒪᒪ ᒐ8'ᒐ#

Printed in Great Britain by
R. & R. Clark Ltd., Edinburgh

CONTENTS

PREFACE

You may be put off by the title of this book. Yet I ask you to read it again carefully. It is not about a 'God who becomes'. God's being is not identified with God's becoming; rather, God's being is ontologically localized.

The somewhat unusual title may at least claim for itself that it does not comprehend God's being from the familiar. At the same time it draws our attention to the fact that many familiar things should be comprehended anew: above all, what 'becoming' means. The becoming in which God's being is, can understandably – or better: in the understanding which comes through faith – signify neither an increase nor a decrease of God's being. Increase and decrease as evaluative categories are better kept far away from the concept of being if we are not to be compelled anew to think of God as the *summum ens* and thus as the supreme value. But the God whose being is in becoming can *die* as a human being! 'Becoming' thus indicates the manner in which God's being exists, and can in so far be understood as the ontological place of God's being.

In order to guard against all misunderstanding let it be here at once stated: the ontological place of God's being, too, is the place of his choice. In that God, however, is understood as the one who chooses, his being is already thought of as a being in becoming. This hermeneutical circle is grounded in an ontological circle which will be designated by the localization 'God's being is in becoming'. The ontological localization of God's being in becoming is an attempt to *think out* theologically how far God *is the living God*. Without the courage to *formulate* the livingness of God, theology will finally become a mausoleum of God's livingness. The God who may be inspected within this mausoleum certainly deserved the protest of Herbert Braun – a protest which as such ought to be heard, however Braun's attempt to think the livingness of God may be judged.

The objections to the title of this book are obvious. But are they valid? Are they *theological* (or not rather traditional metaphysical)objections? Is it theologically true that everything that is in becoming must therefore also have become? Has it already been finally settled that perishing must follow becoming as sunshine follows the rain? The saying of Anaximander is at any rate theologically not absolutely valid. In theology what is called 'becoming' should be understood ontologically, originally as a Trinitarian category, according to which God does not leave his present state behind him as a past in order to proceed towards a future which is unknown to him, but according to which he is in Trinitarian livingness 'undividedly the beginning, succession and end, all at once in his own essence' (cf. Karl Barth, *Church Dogmatics* II/1, p. 615). Thus the title of his book attempts to point to what one could call the axiom of the Christian doctrine of God.

Using a title then which may put people off is a lesser risk than the fact that the following representation aims to be a paraphrase interpreting some trains of thought in Karl Barth's *Church Dogmatics*. Barth himself, however, does not use exactly the same words as in the title of this book. That makes it easy for the critics. But: 'Interpretation means saying *the same thing* in other words' (CD I/1, p. 345). I have tried to do this.

This paraphrase is published because what the following trains of Barth's thought offer to contemporary theology for consideration has remained unnoticed in the present theological debate, both from the side of Herbert Braun as well as – *mirabile dictu* – from the side of Helmut Gollwitzer. Herr Professor Dr. Ernst Fuchs read the manuscript and encouraged me to publish it. Herr Wolf Krötke and Herr Repetent Hans Schreiber were valuable co-workers with me in preparing the manuscript and in much which went beyond technical assistance. My grateful thanks to my teacher and friends, not least to the publisher for his ready willingness to publish it.

EBERHARD JÜNGEL

East Berlin
December 1964

ABBREVIATIONS

CD   Karl Barth's *Church Dogmatics*
EvTh   *Evangelische Theologie*
KuD   *Kerygma und Dogma*
WA   Weimar edition of Luther's collected works
ZKG   *Zeitschrift für Kirchengeschichte*
ZPhF *Zeitschrift für philosophische Forschung*
ZThK *Zeitschrift für Theologie und Kirche*

INTRODUCTION I

THE SITUATION

God's being is discussed. At any rate this description seems to be applicable to the impassioned debate which is being carried on in Protestant theology at the present time. Exponents of this debate today are Herbert Braun[1] and Helmut Gollwitzer.[2] Yet the debate was prepared a long time ago by the works of Karl Barth, Rudolf Bultmann and Friedrich Gogarten. What sense is there in speaking of God? is the question which runs through the whole of Bultmann's writings; it was already asked by him explicitly in 1925[3] and it has expressly determined his thinking right down to his latest publication to date.[4] While Friedrich Gogarten's formulation of the problem is relatively close to that of Bultmann,[5] Barth's formulation is orientated differently. He does not ask what *sense* there is in speaking of God but in what sense we *must* speak of God, so that the speaking is of *God*, and Barth formulates his question from the presupposition that to speak of God is meaningful and possible as 'human speech about God on the basis of an indication by God himself fundamentally transcending all human causation and so devoid of all human basis, merely occurring as a fact and requiring to be acknowledged'.[6] The distinction between the theological

[1] 'Der Sinn der neutestamentlichen Christologie', *Gesammelte Studien zum Neuen Testament und seiner Umwelt* (Tübingen, 1962), p. 243f., and: 'Die Problematik einer Theologie des Neuen Testaments', *Gesammelte Studien*, p. 325f.
[2] *Die Existenz Gottes im Bekenntnis des Glaubens* (Munich, 1963); ET, *The Existence of God as Confessed by Faith* (London, 1965).
[3] *Glauben und Verstehen* I (Tübingen, 1961), p. 26f.; ET, 'What does it mean to speak of God?' in *Faith and Understanding* I (London, 1969), p. 53f.
[4] 'Der Gottesgedanke und der moderne Mensch', *ZThK* 60, 1963, p. 335f.
[5] Characteristic distinctions are likewise certainly not to be mistaken.
[6] *Church Dogmatics* (hereafter abbreviated *CD*) I/1, p. 101. The first volume of Barth's *Die kirchliche Dogmatik* appeared in 1932, being translated

starting-points of Bultmann and Barth may thus be very roughly formulated: with Bultmann the *speech about God* is the proper topic for investigation[7] while with Barth the discussion is about *God's being*.[8] Thereby for both theologians speech about God as Christian speech is bound to the *word of God*.

Helmut Gollwitzer's book on the *Existence of God as confessed by Faith* attempts to show from the viewpoint of a proximity to Barth's theology the consequences of Bultmann's theology with respect to the question of the being of God. From the trend of the Bultmannian theology Gollwitzer perceives the danger that God's being may be thought of as identical with the event in which human existence is transformed by the encounter of God with man, and that 'God' may thus 'be a title for this event and this experience, and that each confession of a real being of God outside of this event is already a fall into an objectivizing metaphysics'.[9] Gollwitzer sees this danger become reality with Herbert Braun, and his book is written to counter this danger.

Two objections above all may be raised against this instructive book.

Firstly: Gollwitzer set the 'necessity of "is" propositions' with reference to God dialectically over against the 'unserviceableness of "is" propositions'[10] with reference to God: 'in view of

---

into English by G. T. Thompson and published in 1936. The remaining volumes I/2–IV/4 appeared through the succeeding years up until 1967, the English translation edited by G. W. Bromily and T. F. Torrance being published from 1956–69. A new translation of I/1 by these editors has now been published (Edinburgh, 1975); all references to CD I/1 refer to this new translation.

[7] That explains the formal pre-eminence of the hermeneutical problem in the theology of Rudolf Bultmann and his pupils.

[8] That explains why as early on as the *Prolegomena der kirchlichen Dogmatik* (1927) statements of dogmatic content take precedence over the hermeneutical difficulties. But cf. also the placing of 'ontic necessity and rationality' before its corresponding 'noetic necessity and rationality' in Barth's interpretation of Anselm (*Fides quaerens intellectum. Anselms Beweis der Existenz Gottes*, Zürich, 1958; ET, Anselm *Fides quaerens intellectum. Anselm's Proof of the Existence of God*, London, 1960), which is fundamental to his *Church Dogmatics*.

[9] *The Existence of God as Confessed by Faith*, p. 34.   [10] *Ibid.* p. 202.

what being means in the worldly sense, God "is" not, and in view of what being means in him, all worldly things have no being', although 'the wonder of the creation consists precisely in the fact that he, who alone "is" from eternity to eternity, calls into being that which "is not" . . . He can condescend to set "alongside" and "outside" of himself other being not identical with himself, and can allow it to live by his free giving – *et tamen Deus manet!*'[11]

The logical difficulties which here arise may be left aside, but we cannot remain silent on one theological difficulty which arises from these statements: In view of what being means in the worldly sense, God 'is' not. But this God 'who is not a part of the history of this world, not a subject within history' nevertheless 'appears, acts and speaks as a subject within history – whereby the word "as" does not mean in the guise of, but in the mode of being of a subject within history'.[12] But then the God who encounters man historically 'in the mode of being of a subject within history', and who therefore 'is', possesses 'no being . . . in view of what being means in him' but rather non-being. It would not be possible then to speak of God's being without speaking of his non-being.

The difficulty is increased when one considers that the being of a subject within history is necessarily *finite being*, that is, mortal being. But if God is in the mode of being of a subject within history then he must possess the attribute of non-being not only 'in view of what being means in him' but also at the same time 'in view of what being means in the worldly sense'. One would then have to say – always in Gollwitzer's sense – that God in the mode of being of a subject within history *has been*.

The difficulty becomes even greater when one takes into account that all speech about the being of God is grounded *Christologically*. Jesus Christ as a 'subject within history' makes speech about God's being possible, because God has been in the mode of being of *this* 'subject within history'. But then all

---

[11] *Ibid*. p. 210. The words 'being' and 'existence' are used by Gollwitzer indiscriminately.   [12] *Ibid*. p. 200.

the problems previously mentioned come to a head in the
Christological question of the significance of the *finite* being of
Jesus Christ and thus the *death* of Jesus Christ for the being of
God. If one wishes to escape from a docetic Christology then
to speak of God's non-being appears unavoidable in face of the
death of Jesus Christ.

One will do well not to defuse this problem too hastily by
pointing to the resurrection of Jesus Christ from the dead, but
precisely here to remember the demand formulated by Gollwitzer (following H. J. Iwand) that 'the question whether
God *is* must "be seen through to the end"'.[13] The Christology
of the Fathers made the attempt to settle the problem which
the death of Jesus Christ posed for the being of God with the
theopaschitic formula: One of the holy Triad has suffered in
the flesh (ἔνα τῆς ἁγίας τριάδος πεπονθέναι σαρκί). And it cannot
be chance that it is precisely the event of the death of Jesus
Christ upon the Cross which calls the *being* of God into question and compels a *Trinitarian* statement of the problem.

Yet before we pursue this pointer and take up a second
objection against Gollwitzer's book, it will be advisable to sum-
marize the first objection. It must be asked whether Gollwitzer's
intention to formulate the being of God historically has been
adequately carried out. Is this indeed the case when God is
thought of in analogy to the human I-thou relationship as a
'Person' who encounters man? Does not a concept of revelation
understood Christologically compel us so to speak of God's

---

[13] *Ibid.* p. 240; cf. H. J. Iwand, 'Glauben und Wissen'. Vorlesung.
Nachgelassene Werke I (Munich, 1962), p. 111. According to Iwand there is
'probably an indirect connection already between revelation' and the fact
that man must 'see the question through to the end, unto its farthest point'
(*ibid.*). Iwand perceives extremely clearly that the consequence of the revelation consists in being able 'to see this question: *An Deus sit?* through to
Gabbatha and Golgotha', but he also sees grounded in just this possibility
the origin of 'something like natural theology' which then 'in divine worship
at the tombstone of the murdered God' celebrates the fact 'that God is "not
an object", not "objective", that he cannot "be there"!' (*ibid.* p. 112). In my
opinion the Christological problem which we defined above has another
more serious dimension than the possibility of the polemic against the claim
that God cannot be objectified, which is indeed a harmless assertion when
advanced as the *final* claim.

being, that the supremely real, in no way merely dialectical, menace of the nothing which threatens God's existence becomes a real theme in the discussion? Is it not precisely a criterion of the Christian understanding of revelation that in revelation God's being is exposed to the *nothing* and only then on the basis of this (on the basis of this, at any rate, without a shadow of doubt) the nothing is also exposed to the being of God? Did not Paul proclaim the resurrected Lord as he who had been crucified (I Cor. 2. 2), precisely on account of that event in which the being of God encountered the nothing? And was not the confession of the Roman centurion: 'Truly this man was the Son of God!' (Mk. 15. 39) elicited, by Jesus crying with a loud voice (an eschatological cry) as he died – nay, by the Jesus who was already *dead*?

Secondly: The other objection which may be raised against Gollwitzer's book appears to be diametrically opposite to the first. For while the first objection was directed towards the *utter weakness* of God's being, which appears in the death of Jesus as the last concrete expression of his 'being in the mode of being of a subject within history', the second objection inquires after the power (*Potenz*) peculiar to God's being and on the ground of which God *is able to be* in the mode of being of a subject within history. Gollwitzer certainly clings to his view *that* God can so exist because 'God's being-for-us is a free unmerited gift which is not grounded in anything that is necessary to God . . . but is grounded in his free, sovereign decision, in his "groundless mercy" for which man can therefore only be utterly thankful.'[14] Therefore according to Gollwitzer we must not evade or shrink from saying also: '*God is in-and-for-himself.*'[15]

Gollwitzer insists on this statement because in God's 'being in-and-for-itself' that 'free, sovereign decision' which is to be understood as 'groundless mercy' is realized. But here the question arises how God's being 'in-and-for-itself' is to be related to his being 'in the mode of being of a subject within history'. Gollwitzer emphasizes that revelation's mode of being,

[14] *The Existence of God*, p. 217.   [15] *Ibid.*

which is definable only with reference to personal-being (in the
relationship of I and thou), has its ground 'not in the essence
of God but in his will', so that it is 'not possible *per analogiam*
to argue back from it to the essence of God in the sense of how
God is constituted, but only to the essence of his will, i.e. from
his will as made known in history to his eternal will as the will
of his free love'.[16]

   This sentence is surprising. Gollwitzer, following Karl Barth
– the context makes that clear – wants to avoid an *'analogia
entis'* in favour of an *'analogia relationis'*.[17] We must now ask,
however, whether that can be attained in this way. Is there
not just here a metaphysical background – which is quite in-
different towards God's acts of revelation in history – introduced into the being of God by this distinction between the
essence and will of God in the 'essence of God – in the sense
of how God is constituted' – which is distinguished from the
'essence of his will'?

   It is clear that Gollwitzer *does not want to say* this. But can this
consequence be avoided if the 'essence of his will' which is
understood as God's free love is not at the same time understood as the *will of his essence*?[18] Is not God's essence *determined*
just in his will? Is not precisely God's 'eternal will as the will
of his free love' directed to his revelation by virtue of his free
decision as Lord which in such love determines his being and
essence? Does not the *being* of God which becomes manifest in
and as history compel us to think of God's being in its power
(*Kraft*) which makes revelation possible, *already* as historical
being? And can we think in a historical sense of God's being
in its power (*Potenz*) which makes possible historical revelation
otherwise than as Trinitarian being? If we want to think of
God's being in-and-for-itself, as postulated by Gollwitzer, in a
Christian manner, i.e. in conformity with revelation, *must* we

---

[16] *Ibid.* p. 186.   [17] *Ibid.* p. 185.
[18] Cf. on the other hand Karl Barth, according to whom 'God himself does
not exist otherwise and therefore will not and must not be understood otherwise than in this concrete livingness (sc. of his decision), in the determination of his will, *which as such* is also a determination of his being' (*CD* II/2,
p. 79; my addition and italics).

not then think of this being as being which, in a certain way, is already in advance of history, in that God as Father, Son and Spirit is already so to speak 'ours in advance'?[19] The historical power of God's revelation which stooped down even to the acceptance of the utter weakness of death (ἐσταυρώθη ἐξ ἀσθενείας (he was crucified through weakness), 2 Cor. 13. 4) must have already been grounded in the pre-historical power (*Potenz*) of the being of God as Father, Son and Spirit.

The two objections which have been raised here against Gollwitzer's book take us back to the question as to why Gollwitzer decided not to define the being of God in a Trinitarian way from the outset and to see the thesis of the historicality of God's being through to the end precisely within this Trinitarian definition. The indication that only 'some things, by no means all things, that would have to be said'[20] for the purpose of clarifying the sense of 'Christian talk about the existence and reality of God' may be stated, is hardly able to explain this renunciation of Trinitarian definition in speaking of God's being, when this definition is supposed to be dogmatically fundamental for the Christian concept of God's being. Gollwitzer's indication, which is to be understood as a criticism, that 'Kant had no use for the doctrine of the Trinity'[21] allows us to infer that Gollwitzer himself holds the Trinitarian definition of the Christian concept of God as indispensable.

Gollwitzer's book stimulates us to recover what is there neglected. In the following pages I would like to do this along with an interpretation of the corresponding train of Karl Barth's thought. In this respect Barth's *Church Dogmatics*, which is frequently cited by Gollwitzer, provides at the same time an implicit critique of Gollwitzer's own interesting book *The Existence of God as Confessed by Faith*.

The following interpretation of Barth's exposition of the being of God limits itself to Barth's *Church Dogmatics* and executes this task in the form of a paraphrase of Karl Barth's train of thought. If contemporary theologians let themselves

---

[19] K. Barth, *CD* I/1, p, 383. Cf. *CD* I/2, p. 34.
[20] Gollwitzer, *op. cit.* p. 202.   [21] *Ibid.* p. 73, fn. 1.

B

be encouraged by such a paraphrase to listen seriously and cordially to one another and to combine the necessary criticism of other positions with the readiness to test critically their own starting-points, then much would be achieved. If, however, beyond this, this kind of paraphrase makes plain in how far the hermeneutical study, in which my teacher Ernst Fuchs has trained us, is seeking to give Barth's writings the understanding that is their due, then I shall be very pleased. Such an understanding remains essential to the Protestant theology of our time – a time which so far as dogmatic theology is concerned, appears to have grown tired.

INTRODUCTION II:

RESPONSIBLE SPEECH ABOUT THE BEING OF GOD ACCORDING TO KARL BARTH

Barth thinks as a theologian. This sentence, which appears trivial, loses all triviality when one considers that for Barth 'to think as a theologian' can mean nothing else than 'to think consistently and exclusively as a theologian'. What that signifies is shown by his question concerning the being of God. This question does not itself arise out of questioning; neither does it invent a problem which sooner or later faces the more or less radical questioning that calls something or everything into question. The theological question concerning the being of God *reflects* on the being of God. This means, however, that the being of God which is the subject of theological inquiry *precedes* the question.[1] The predicate is to be taken strictly. God's being *precedes* the theological inquiry after this being; it is not in any way *presupposed* by this inquiry. All really radical questioning sets aside human presuppositions. Furthermore, where it was asserted (and thus thought and exposed to questioning) that God's being was the presupposition of thinking (and therewith of questioning), just here there was always a questioning (and thinking and asserting) which saw itself obliged to ignore *this* human presupposition. The being of God as object of theological questioning cannot be such a presupposition. Much more does this being so precede all theological questioning that in its course it paves the way for questioning and first of all brings the questioning on to the path of thinking. Upon this path the question reflects upon the

[1] *CD* I/2, pp. 5-7.

being of God. The being of God has thus prevenient character.[2] The path upon which the question concerning the being of God is brought by God himself, is no common path. Barth emphatically rejected the opinion that theology has to do with a general way of thinking. Such an opinion would just simply misunderstand that the theological question concerning the being of God has been brought on to a path along which the being of God has *itself proceeded* and which thereby first of all was paved and made into a path. The path upon which the question concerning the being of God has been directed and along which it must proceed is thus a special path. The theological concept with which this special path is properly comprehended is called revelation.

The claim that the *being* of God *precedes* (human questioning) strikes us as strange. This strangeness may not be defused by describing the manner of speaking of which we have availed ourselves as anthropomorphic or mythological. Nothing would thereby be explained and the problem would only be rendered harmless. Over against this it seems more necessary to set oneself in the sphere of this strangeness so that it may be comprehended *as* strangeness. This strangeness might then turn out to be something precious. In the following pages an attempt will be made to elucidate what it means that the being of God proceeds, and thus precedes all human questioning. In this attempt we confront the hermeneutical problem in its most concentrated form while we turn our thought to the doctrine of God. The being of God is the hermeneutical problem of theology. More exactly: the fact that the being of God *proceeds* is precisely the hermeneutical problem. For only because the being of God proceeds is there an encounter between God and

[2] When Thomas Bonhoeffer (*Die Gotteslehre des Thomas von Aquin als Sprachproblem*, Tübingen, 1961, p. 3) says that theology is 'demanded where speech about God's word has become customary, without God's word itself becoming actual' we would add that theology is made possible where the speech about God's word is customary as speech about the being of God, because the being of God became actual as the word of God. Theology *can* proceed along the path of thinking when it follows the word of God. But it must itself proceed along this path and itself confront all the difficulties which obstruct this path.

man. And the hermeneutical problem is grounded precisely in this encounter between God and man which owes its origin to the movement of God's being. The encounter between God and man which owes its origin to the movement of God's being is, according to Barth, first and above all the encounter between the electing God and the elected man which is fulfilled in Jesus Christ. Thus the existence of the man Jesus confronts us with the hermeneutical problem, both with respect to the understanding of God as well as with respect to the understanding of the self and the world: 'At no level or time can we have to do with God without having also to do with this man. We cannot conceive ourselves and the world without first conceiving this man with God as the witness of the gracious purpose with which God willed and created ourselves and the world and in which we may exist in it and with it.'[3]

[3] *CD*, IV/2, p. 33.

1

━━◆━━

GOD'S BEING REVEALED

If we treat the claim, 'God's being *proceeds*', in Barth's sense, seriously, then we shall have to begin our question concerning the being of God not with the doctrine of God in the narrower sense, but there where the special way of God's being as revelation is comprehended. That takes place doubtless in the Christology of the *Church Dogmatics*, which therefore on this account not only determines the *whole Dogmatics* but accompanies it in the form of fundamental paragraphs. That part of the *Church Dogmatics* which especially deals with Christology is the doctrine of reconciliation. In *Church Dogmatics IV* the subject matter which we have summarized with the phrase 'God's being proceeds', is designated with two formally corresponding headings: in connection with the orthodox doctrines of *status exinanitionis* and *status exaltationis* Barth speaks of the '*Way* of the Son of God into the Far Country' under the chapter-heading 'Jesus Christ, the Lord as Servant' and of the '*Homecoming* of the Son of Man' under the reversed chapter-heading 'Jesus Christ, the Servant as Lord'.[1] 'The Way of the

---

[1] Barth thus co-ordinates the classical doctrine *de statibus Christi* with that of the *triplex munus Christi*. The *munus sacerdotale* (Jesus Christ, the Lord as Servant) has been co-ordinated with the *status exinanitionis*, the *munus regale* (Jesus Christ, the Servant as Lord) with the *status exaltationis*. As object of theological knowledge, however, the *munus propheticum* (Jesus Christ, the true witness) along with Christ's offices, which are connected by the two '*status*', is no extension of the 'essential knowledge of the act of reconciliation' but designates the dimension of the revelation of the act of reconciliation which is *not* to be separated from the act. 'For as it takes place in its perfection, and with no need of supplement, it also expresses, discloses, mediates and *reveals* itself' (*CD* IV/3, 1, p. 8). One can well formulate it: the prophetic office of Jesus Christ unveils the being of Jesus Christ in his work

Son of God into the Far Country' and the 'Homecoming of
the Son of Man' bring the *movement* of God's being to manifestation. But they so bring this movement to manifestation
that the origin of all the ways of God thereby becomes recognizable. This origin is one which takes place in the being of God
itself, an origin which is in no way *strange* to God. Barth speaks,
therefore, of God's 'primal decision'[2] which is perfected in
God's eternal election of grace. The Christology of the doctrine
of reconciliation, therefore, points necessarily back to the
doctrine of election. God preceded the far country into which

---

of reconciliation as language-event. For 'reconciliation is not a dark or dumb
but a perspicuous and vocal event. It is not closed in upon itself, but moves
out and communicates itself. It is event only as it expresses, discloses and
mediates itself, as it is not merely real but also true, and as true as it is real'
(*CD* IV/3, 1, p. 8; here is to be found Barth's starting-point for overcoming
the 'subject-object-*schema*').
   In the face of such sentences which stand in no way isolated in the *Church
Dogmatics* it is not really intelligible why Barth in his *Einführung in die
evangelische Theologie* (Zürich, 1962) p. 198; ET, *Evangelical Theology: An
Introduction* (London, 1963) p. 182, somewhat gruffly banishes the category
of the language-event – a category so relevant to the problems treated by
him in the *munus propheticum* – to the realm of practical theology. 'The special
problem-area of practical theology is what is today somewhat bombastically
termed the "*language-event*". This is then customarily – and quite unsuitably
– presented as the basic problem of exegesis, and, where possible, also of
dogmatics' (p. 182). Language-event is (at any rate for Ernst Fuchs) a
Christological category which as such has also general hermeneutical
significance. It therefore actually has its place in the basic problems of
exegesis and dogmatics, assuming that in exegesis and dogmatics the fundamental issue concerns the word of God. But if in the category of the language-
event it is a question of comprehending God's word as event (and thus God's
revelation as mystery), then we shall scarcely be able to compare appropriately this care with that *ars amandi* which would always be given the pre-
eminence over against 'a true, juicy love-story'. No, if theology did not learn
it from Hegel then it should at least have let itself be reminded by Karl
Barth 'that the source of knowledge of Reformation theology had been the
word, the word of God, the word of truth. But this also means, the event of
God, the event of truth . . . an event at which he for whom it is to be an
event must be present; an event which by repetition, and by man's renewal
of his presence, must ever become event anew' (Karl Barth, *Die Protestantische Theologie im 19. Jahrhundert*, Zürich, 1952, p. 373; ET, *Protestant Theology
in the Nineteenth Century*, London, 1972, p. 416). So then, why not language-
event?
   [2] *CD* IV/2, p. 32, and above all, *CD* II/2, p. 9, and elsewhere.

he went, in that he decided to go there. This precedence of God in his primal decision shows that God's being not only 'proceeds' on the way into the far country but that God's being is *in motion* from eternity. God's being is moved being: 'Being in the act of his revelation.'[3] At the same time, however, God's primal decision teaches us to understand God's *being concretely*. God's primal decision to take the way into the far country is certainly not a decision forced upon him from the far country, no decision which is *strange* to him, but his own *free* decision. Moreover, this decision as his decision to take the way into the far country in which God *endures* what is strange to him for the benefit of man threatened in the strange land, is an act of *love*. Thus God in his primal decision which is realized in our history allows us to perceive 'God's being as he who loves in freedom'.[4] The doctrine of election necessarily points back to the doctrine of God in the narrower sense. At the same time the doctrine of election also points back to the doctrine of the Trinity in the *Church Dogmatics*. For God's way into the far country is indeed the way of the *Son* of God; in that primal decision in the unity of the *Spirit* between the *Father* who sends the Son upon this way, and the Son who was obedient, the Son was appointed to become one with the man Jesus. Thus God's moved being will certainly have to be treated – and especially in the doctrine of the Trinity – as a being moved by *God*. Therefore we need not wonder that Barth's doctrine of the Trinity is found at the beginning of his *Church Dogmatics*. For the doctrine of the Trinity provides 'an answer to the question of the *God* who reveals himself in revelation'.[5]

However, because revelation concerns the being of God, assuming that it is God who reveals himself, the doctrine of the Trinity is 'a constituent part, the decisive part of the . . . doctrine of God'.[6] This part is decisive because the doctrine of the Trinity fundamentally distinguishes 'the Christian doctrine of God as Christian' and 'the Christian concept of revelation as Christian in contrast to all other possible doctrines of God or

³ *CD* II/1, p. 257. ⁴ *CD* II/1, p. 257.
⁵ *CD* I/1, pp. 311–12. ⁶ *CD* II/1, p. 312.

concepts of revelation'.[7] Because for Barth the 'problem of the doctrine of the Trinity' necessarily confronts us from out of the Bible, when we inquire after the being of God with 'the question put to the Bible about revelation',[8] then the solution of this problem is also decisive for the Christian concept of revelation and thus the understanding of the being of God. Therefore Barth sets the doctrine of the Trinity at the beginning of his *Dogmatics*[9] in order that 'its content be decisive and controlling for the whole of dogmatics'.[10]

This positioning, which allows the doctrine of the Trinity to stand at the introduction of the whole *Church Dogmatics*, is a *hermeneutical* decision of the greatest relevance. That shows itself formally in that the doctrine of the Trinity is to be found in the Prolegomena, thus precisely where one expects the treatment of the hermeneutical problems. For Barth also the

[7] *CD* I/1, p. 301.

[8] *CD* I/1, p. 303.

[9] As, by the way, Peter Lombard had already done in his 'Sentences', for which he was censured by Matthias Joseph Scheeben (*Handbuch der katholischen Dogmatik*. Erstes Buch: Theologische Erkenntnislehre, ed. by Martin Grabmann, 2nd ed. Freiburg, 1948, p. 455), 'that in the doctrine of God the doctrine of the essence of God is not accentuated and treated at the beginning . . . and that the concrete subsistence of God [in three Persons] is immediately discussed'. The arrangement of the Lombardian 'Sentences' which subsumes the doctrine of God in general under the doctrine of the Trinity was first broken up by Thomas Aquinas who first of all treats 'those things pertaining to the divine essence' (*ea, quae ad essentiam divinam pertinent*) (S.th.I, qu. 2–26) and only then in the next part turns himself to 'those things pertaining to the distinction of the persons' (*ea, quae pertinent ad distinctionem Personarum*) (S.th. I, qu. 27–43). This division in dogmatics has prevailed in Catholic theology (apart from a few 'noteworthy exceptions') down to our present day, a fact which Karl Rahner expressly regrets ('Kleine Bemerkungen zum dogmatischen Traktat "De Trinitate"', *Theologisches Jahrbuch*, ed. A. Dänhardt, Leipzig, 1964, p. 97f.; ET, 'Remarks on the Dogmatic Treatise "De Trinitate"', *Theological Investigations* IV, London, 1966, p. 77f.). Rahner's statement that the division of the doctrine of God – which is not yet clearly drawn in the *Summa* commonly attributed to Alexander of Hales – into two treatises, which was accomplished 'first in Thomas from motives not yet really explained' (p. 83), may be supplemented by a reference to Thomas Bonhoeffer's interpretation of Aquinas's doctrine of God (*Die Gotteslehre des Thomas von Aquin als Sprachproblem*, above all §19–21).

[10] *CD* I/1, p. 303.

hermeneutical problems – in spite of other misleading statements – are in no way more or less unpleasant preliminary questions. The insight that without 'anticipating material dogmas' neither a doctrine of Scripture nor, even less, a doctrine of the word of God can be formulated,[11] may rather be urged as evidence that just where Barth decides in a hermeneutical way about the construction of the *Dogmatics* with respect to both organization and content, he sees himself compelled at that point to decide about the hermeneutic itself, according to which the construction of the *Dogmatics* shall be decided. The placing of the doctrine of the Trinity at the beginning of the *Church Dogmatics* is therefore a hermeneutical decision of the greatest relevance because on the one hand the whole *Church Dogmatics* finds its hermeneutical foundation here; on the other hand with just this decision the hermeneutics itself finds its own starting point. It is worth while illustrating this point by elucidating Barth's reflections on the 'root of the doctrine of the Trinity'. We shall proceed by first turning our attention to Barth's resistance to the different variations of the *vestigia trinitatis* as possible roots of the doctrine of the Trinity, in order then to apply ourselves to the detailed statements about the real root (in Barth's sense) of the doctrine of the Trinity.

(a) *The* vestigium trinitatis *as a hermeneutical problem*

The problem of the *vestigium trinitatis* is posed by the history of the dogma of the Trinity. In the Fathers, in Scholasticism, in the Reformers (Luther – 'in his table talk at least'[12]) and in the more recent theology, both Protestant and Catholic, attempts have been made in an abundance of variations to exhibit a similarity between certain structures of created reality and the structure of the being of God understood from a Trinitarian point of view. It was thought possible to discover

[11] *CD* I/1, p. 43.
[12] *CD* I/1, p. 336, and incidentally, not only in his table talk but also in his preaching (cf. WA 4, pp. 597, 600, 602).

'an essential trinitarian disposition supposedly immanent in some created realities quite apart from their possible conscription by God's revelation' as 'traces of the trinitarian Creator God in being as such'.[13] When one acknowledges that there are such *vestigia trinitatis* and that they are recognizable as such, then the problem arises whether these are not to be seen as the root of the doctrine of the Trinity. This problem is 'of the greatest importance, not only for the question of the root of the *doctrine of the Trinity*, but for that of *revelation generally*, for that of the grounding of theology in revelation alone, and finally even for that of the meaning and possibility of theology . . .'.[14] Without doubt, we are concerned here with a hermeneutical problem.

After his review of the 'material' which was utilized for the purpose of defending the *vestigia trinitatis*, Barth expresses the impression that 'there must be "something in" the connection between the Trinity and all the "trinities" to which reference is made here. . . . The only question is what.'[15] This question is then discussed by him as a problem – no, as 'the problem of *theological language*'.[16]

If one takes seriously the assurances of the Church Fathers and Scholastics that the real perception of *vestigia trinitatis* can take place only *trinitate posita*,[17] that one has not to understand God from what he has done, but the things he has done, from God (*Deum ex factis, sed ea, quae facta sunt, ex Deo*),[18] then one will have to grant them that for all the trouble they took to discover *vestigia trinitatis* they were 'in search of language for the mystery of God which was known to them by revelation'.[19] In the sense of their search for the right language, there is 'something in' their effort. For 'theology and the Church, and even the Bible itself, speak no other language than the language of this world' on the presupposition 'that in this language God's revelation *might* be referred to, witness *might* be given, God's word *might* be proclaimed, dogma *might* be

---

[13] *CD* I/1, p. 334.   [14] *CD* I/1, p. 335.   [15] *CD* I/1, p. 339.
[16] *CD* I/1, p. 341.   [17] Thomas Aquinas, S.th. I, qu. 32 art. 1.
[18] Irenaeus, *Adv. haer.* II, 37, 1.   [19] *CD* I/1, p. 340.

formulated and declared'.[20] According to Barth, what marks out 'the discoverers of the *vestigia trinitatis*' in this their common oneness with the Bible, the Church and every theology, is that in that they spoke the language of this world they were seeking *in* this language the language for the Trinitarian mystery of God. Thereby theology is confronted with the question of the *capacity* of language. For the decisive question for Barth in his debate with the 'discoverers' of the *vestigia trinitatis* is whether the capacity to speak about God in the language of the world 'is to be understood as a capability *inherent* in the language and thus in the world, i.e. in man, or as an act of daring *demanded* of the language and so of the world or man, so to speak, from without'.[21]

The question is then: what capability does language possess? Barth always presupposes here that it is a question concerning the language 'shaped in form and content by the creaturely nature of the world and also conditioned by the limitations of humanity: the language in which man as he is, as sinful and corrupt man, wrestles with the world as it encounters him and as he sees and tries to understand it'.[22] Is this language capable of grasping revelation? The fact that revelation is spoken about in this language, and indeed appropriately spoken about, cannot be disputed. The dispute concerns the *possibility* of this fact.

In that the possibility in this sense is disputed, in that it is not only asked *how* one shall speak about God's revelation but what makes such speech about revelation possible, we pass beyond the horizon of the problem of a hermeneutic which is orientated about the relationship by which sounds, words and things are designated and which therefore is essentially a hermeneutic of signification.[23] More is at stake when it is

---

[20] *CD* I/1, p. 339.   [21] *CD* I/1, p. 339.   [22] *CD* I/1, p. 339.

[23] By a hermeneutic of signification is meant a doctrine of understanding embracing the ontological distinction between 'thing' (*res*) and 'sign' (*signa*). The tradition of this distinction is old. In Augustine we read: 'All teaching is either of things or of signs; but things are learnt by signs' (*Omnis doctrina vel rerum est vel signorum; sed res per signa discuntur*) (*De doctrina christiana* 1. Book II, 2). Cf. in addition the brilliant treatment by R.

maintained 'not that the language could grasp the revelation but that revelation . . . could grasp the language'.[24] Thus theology moves within a sphere of problems which is hermeneutically determined by the antithesis of *analogia entis* and *analogia fidei*. At any rate this is how Barth understands it when he fears that the teaching of the *vestigia trinitatis* concerns – probably against the intention of its discoverers – 'a genuine *analogia entis*'.[25, 26]

Lorenz: 'Die Wissenschaftslehre Augustins' (ZKG, 4th series, vol. 67 (1955/6), pp. 29f. and 213f.). The beginnings of a hermeneutic of signification are already prepared in Parmenides; cf. E. Fink, *Zur ontologischen Frühgeschichte von Raum-Zeit-Bewegung* (The Hague, 1957) above all p. 53f.; E. Jüngel, *Zum Ursprung der Analogie bei Parmenides und Heraklit* (Berlin, 1964). With regard to this problem cf. also Thomas Bonhoeffer (*Die Gotteslehre des Thomas von Aquin*, p. 124, fn. 4), who aptly distinguishes between a 'hermeneutic of signification' and a 'hermeneutic of reiteration [Wiederholung]'.

[24] *CD* I/1, p. 340.   [25] *CD* I/1, p. 334.

[26] Cf. also *CD* I/1, p. 335: 'The question is whether these *vestigia trinitatis*, in virtue of the conclusions that are to be drawn from this acknowledgment . . . do not compel us to pass over first to the easy double track of "revelation" and "primal revelation" (P. Althaus) and then very quickly from this half-measure to the genuine Roman Catholic theology of the *analogia entis*.'

In the face of such statements it may surprise us that K. Barth in his doctrine of reconciliation (*CD* IV/3) made the attempt to win back again a 'clear and unequivocal sense' for the discussion of the problem which has been characterized with the concept 'primal revelation' or 'revelation of creation' (*CD* IV/3, p. 140). What is meant here? Barth will put it on account that the act of reconciliation in Jesus Christ took place as history in a specific 'sphere', in a specific 'location' (p. 151). This sphere is the creation, 'God's creaturely world' (p. 137). The creation is the *good* work of the creator. As a good work God preserves his creation. He preserves it – in spite of man's sin which destroys it – *through to the end* because he has determined it to the location and sphere in which the reconciliation shall take place. The 'work of his creative grace has in view his reconciling work' (p. 138). This relationship between creation and reconciliation (covenant) was so defined in *CD* III/1 that the creation is 'the external basis of the covenant which conversely is its internal basis' (*CD* IV/3, p. 137). The doctrine of reconciliation, however, has not only to consider what this relationship means for the reconciliation, but also what it means for the *creation*.

God, on the basis of his reconciling work, is 'the Guarantor, Sustainer and Protector of his creaturely world' (p. 138). 'To the *faithfulness* of the Creator . . . there corresponds the *persistence* and *constancy* of the creature' (p. 138). This constancy, however, does not rest in itself. And the creaturely world expresses *in its own way* that what it is in its constancy did not arise out of

It is of significance for what follows that Barth agrees with
the teachers of the *vestigia trinitatis* that starting from revelation

---

itself. This language is its own testimony. But just as the creation owes its
existence to the faithfulness of the Creator, so it owes to him 'also this its
language . . . Like its persistence, its self-witness and lights are not extin-
guished by the corruption of the relationship between God and man through
the sin of man, his pride and sloth and falsehood' (p. 139). The language of
this self-witness of the creaturely world is, to be sure, first discovered
through God's own self-revelation in Jesus Christ and stamped as the
language of the *created* world; but just as such it is in no way silenced by the
language of revelation. This language is, indeed, not God's self-revelation;
nevertheless the revelations of the creature, the κτίσις itself (p. 140), take
place within it (in a limiting sense).

Of what does such 'self-witness of the creature' speak? It speaks of the
'quality of divinely created terrestrial being' (p. 141), of 'lights', 'words'
and 'truths' which the intelligible cosmos makes known to the intelligent
creature. In the 'converse of the cosmos with itself' (p. 142) the order,
structure and constancy of the world created by God become visible as the
truth of the world created by God. This worldly, not divine, truth is the
'obstacle to the onrush of chaos into the terrestrial life' (p. 141), i.e. it shows
'that the Creator is faithful to his creature' (p. 153). There must be a 'sharp'
distinction here: 'In themselves' those truths and those lights of the cosmos
have 'nothing to do with God as the Founder and Lord of his covenant with
man' (p. 151), they are 'no covenant of God with man' (p. 143), they can,
however, in the light of the one revelation of God be set in a relationship
with the covenant (p. 157 cf. p. 159). The *enabling* of this relationship is the
'irrevocable', 'prototypal' word of God (cf. p. 160), from which these – in relation to God's self-witness – so problematical and relative self-witnesses of the
creature *receive* the 'highest practical value, force and significance' (p. 163),
as they 'reflect God's eternal light, as they answer his word and as they *correspond* to his truth' (p. 164; my italics). The 'change of form . . . which takes
place with the self-declaration of God' (p. 157) can *make* the self-witnesses of
the cosmos – of the world – into 'parables of the kingdom of heaven' (pp. 112,
115, 117 and elsewhere). Certainly it is true that 'the world as such can
produce no parables of the kingdom of heaven!' (p. 143). Yet because the
whole creation as the 'external basis of the covenant' is determined by God
to be 'the theatre of his dominion and therefore the recipient and bearer of
his word' (p. 117), it is all the more true that 'in the world reconciled by
God in Jesus Christ there is no secular sphere abandoned by him or with-
drawn from his control' (p. 119). God causes the secular sphere to *become* the
parable of his word, to become a 'true word' that is 'laid upon the lips' of the
godless creature (p. 125). The secular sphere speaks *of* God because God
speaks *to* it and causes it to speak of itself and at the same time, of God. It is
to be observed that this language is not the capacity of the world, but the
'capacity of Jesus Christ' (p. 118). The capacity of Jesus Christ, however,
goes beyond the so-called 'sphere of the Bible and the Church' (p. 117) and

'enough elements could be found' in the language 'to be able to speak about revelation . . . but still to some extent intelligibly

causes men 'quite apart from and even in the face of their own knowledge or volition' to speak 'words which can seriously be called true' (p. 118), so that 'even from the mouth of Balaam, the well-known voice of the Good Shepherd may sound, and it is not to be ignored in spite of its sinister origin' (p. 119). The Church has to 'eavesdrop in the world at large' (p. 117), to listen to the words which have been so qualified – to the free communications of Jesus Christ (pp. 131, 133, and elsewhere) – to separate them critically, test and distinguish them (p. 125f.). Parables of the kingdom of heaven are no 'special source of revelation' (p. 133), they do not serve as the foundation of a dogma about it, but stand in the service 'of the awakening power of the universal prophecy of Jesus Christ' in which they 'have their final origin and meaning' (pp. 128–9).

Has not Karl Barth thus nevertheless followed that 'easy double track of "revelation" and "primal revelation" '? Scarcely. What he wanted to say was this alone, that God's revelation does not take place apart from the creation which was determined as the sphere of revelation, just as Jesus Christ speaks the language of the world in order that man may hear and understand him. But if Jesus Christ can speak intelligibly in this language, then the language of the world has its own truth and worth which consists precisely in its being the language of the world created by God.

In spite of Barth's formulation (*CD* IV/2, p. 725) it would certainly be wiser not to assert that Barth, with the above statements, has revived the Patristic teaching of the *logos spermatikos* (against G. Koch: 'Gotteserkenntnis ohne Christus?' *EvTh* 23, 1963, p. 584). What Carl-Heinz Ratschow in his otherwise so valuable dogmatic study *Gott existiert* (p. 63f.) puts forward concerning the interpretation of *CD* IV/3, pp. 110–65, passes by Barth's own intention with an assurance which makes us marvel. That the current opinion about the dogmatics of the old Protestant orthodoxy requires a revision is convincingly shown by Ratschow in his fascinating analysis of the Lutheran orthodoxy. And Barth's protest in matters *notitia dei naturalis* which he urged over against the old Protestant orthodoxy is to be corrected historically or at least to be more carefully formulated. If it is true that 'in the 17th century there was scarcely a theologian' who wanted to say *more* about the problem of the *notitia dei naturalis* than Barth in *CD* IV/3, we would still have to take into consideration that Barth protested against the beginnings of those things in the old Protestant Fathers which he set out to combat in the 20th century. And after a thorough examination of the subject matter one would scarcely be able to maintain that Barth, in the outline presented in *CD* IV/3, has 'fundamentally changed his views in these questions'. As regards the old Protestant orthodoxy historical faithfulness compels us to note that in spite of a number of historical errors of judgment which have crept in, few have done so much for the theological evaluation of those theologians as Barth. It is absolutely clear that he has gone into *their* school with much attention and love. Cf. Ratschow, *Gott existiert. Eine dogmatische Studie* (Berlin, 1966).

and perspicuously'.[27] He perceives in the 'more or less felicitous discoveries of *vestigia' trinitatis* an 'expression . . . of confidence in the *capacity of revelation over reason*'.[28] In so far it is not a question of an *'analogia entis'* but rather of the thoroughly legitimate 'attempt to speak theological language'.[29] The problem of making such an attempt to speak theological language consists in the fact that this language 'can only be the language of the world' which, however, 'must . . . at root always speak *contrary* to the natural capacity of this language, must speak of God's revelation *in* this language as *theological* language.'[30] Revelation cannot be brought to speech 'by a possibility of logical construction'.[31] In Barth's sense that would be just an *analogia entis*. But the language in which the revelation shall be able to come to speech must, 'as it were, be commandeered'[32] by revelation. Where such 'commandeering' of the language by revelation for revelation becomes event, then there is a *gain to language*. It consists in the fact that God as God comes to speech. Over against this, in the reverse case, one would have to speak of a *loss of revelation* if revelation is commandeered by language on the pattern of the *analogia entis per analogiam nominum*.[33] This loss consists in the fact that God does not come to speech as God but as *nomen*.[34] The

[27] *CD* I/1, p. 340.   [28] *CD* I/1, p. 341.   [29] *CD* I/1, p. 341.
[30] *CD* I/1, p. 341.   [31] *CD* I/1, p. 346.   [32] *CD* I/1, p. 340.

[33] By *analogia nominum* we understand that venture which from certain presuppositions claims the power to capture revelation from language. Presupposed thereby is:
(a) that language consists mainly of *nomina*,
(b) that the *nomina* stand in a sense-structure,
(c) that this sense-structure presents a coherent standard of reference,
(d) that this coherent standard of reference is constituted by signification.
Cf. Marcel Reding, 'Analogia entis und analogia nominum', *EvTh* 23, 1963, p. 225f. Thomas Bonhoeffer, *Die Gotteslehre des Thomas von Aquin als Sprachproblem*, p. 135, points out the consequence: 'In a language which interprets its interpretation of the world as timelessly valid for the truth of its "*species intelligibilis*" in which time is overlooked, one appeals to a "*species intelligibilis*" in which the time is surveyed . . . This one "*species intelligibilis*" is no concept of God . . . but the attack on God in which language has appropriated to itself the right to eternity.'
[34] The pseudotheological attempt (repulsed by Barth) to bring revelation to speech through the possibility of a logical construction has a correspond-
C

antithesis of *analogia entis* and *analogia fidei* can accordingly be so characterized: *analogia entis* (*nominum*) leads to a loss of revelation; *analogia fidei* leads to a gain to language, to the possibility of theological speech about God.

It is a question, here and there, of an analogy. And in so far we now have to ask what guards theology in its necessary use of analogy (which in the attempt to investigate theological language seems to be clearly not only unavoidable, but even indispensable) from placing revelation and language in a false relationship and thus speaking inappropriately of revelation. According to Barth, revelation is spoken of inappropriately when the revelation is not *interpreted* but *illustrated*. For 'revelation will submit only to interpretation and not to illustration'.[35] The appropriate relationship between revelation and language is therefore that of interpretation. It is thus clear from the foregoing discussion that the interpretation of revelation by language is an event in which language is 'commandeered' by

---

ence in myth in so far as this, with Bultmann, is understood as a human attempt to speak 'of the other world in terms of this world, and of the gods in terms derived from human life' (*Kerygma und Mythos I*, p. 22; ET, *Kerygma and Myth* I, p. 10). Bultmann's statement, that 'myth contains elements which demand its own criticism – namely, its imagery with its apparent claim to objective validity. The real purpose of myth is to speak of a transcendent power which controls the world and man, but that purpose is impeded and obscured by the terms in which it is expressed' (*ibid.* p. 23; ET, p. 22), is true for myths generally, and in so far represents no specific problem for Christian theology (as the fragments of Xenophanes and Heraclitus show). This theological statement is relevant also in Bultmann's sense only in so far as in the New Testament the attempt was made to bring revelation to speech in mythological words. The motive for the criticism of the myth springs here out of myth only in so far as the mythological speech of the New Testament speaks of revelation. In so far demythologization as a theological task is basically differentiated from the consequence of a criticism of myth which results from the myth itself. Demythologization as a theological task can only be the interpreting reiteration of the capture of language through revelation, whereby the mythological element of the myth as an attempt to capture revelation through language is repulsed. Bultmann's programme of demythologizing presupposes the theological insight that the New Testament texts as proclamations are composed in language captured by revelation but which as human speech of their time have not remained free from the contrary movement.

[35] *CD* I/1, p. 345.

revelation, that the interpretation of revelation is thus an act of daring which is '*demanded* of language from outside it'.[36] At the same time, however, this demand on language will have to be understood in such a way that revelation grants *courage* to speak of God, so that interpretation is possible.

This courage which is granted to language by revelation as a demand on language is, however, to be strictly distinguished from the '*desire* to illustrate revelation'.[37] The desire to illustrate does not spring from the demand on language but from language's own capability. Barth knows extremely well that there is 'no interpretation of revelation – not excepting the most careful dogmatics and even Church dogma itself – which does not contain elements of illustration'.[38] Nevertheless, for him 'the *desire* to illustrate revelation, let alone the claim that illustration is *essential*, let alone the assertion that this or that *is* an illustration of revelation', is tantamount to 'a desertion of revelation' and thus 'unbelief'.[39]

The teaching of the *vestigia trinitatis* is for Barth the illegitimate transition from the interpretation to the illustration of revelation, a transition which should 'obviously not take place in the language of theology'.[40] Therefore he rejects 'the teaching of the *vestigia*'.[41]

The relationship between interpretation and illustration requires further explanation. Barth's informative statement, 'Interpretation means saying *the same thing* in other words. Illustration means saying the same thing *in other words*'[42], is certainly not exhaustive, but points in a definite direction. It is clearly a problem of the *sameness* of revelation. Interpretation protects the sameness of revelation in that it brings revelation (and only this) *as* revelation to speech. Illustration endangers the sameness of revelation in that it brings *with* revelation *also* language (*nomina*) as revelation to speech. But where also language (*nomina*) as revelation is brought to speech along with revelation, revelation is no longer protected as revelation *and*

[36] *CD* I/1, p. 339.   [37] *CD* I/1, p. 345.   [38] *CD* I/1, p. 345.
[39] *CD* I/1, p. 345.   [40] *CD* I/1, p. 345.
[41] *CD* I/1, p. 346.   [42] *CD* I/1, p. 345.

language no longer as language.[43] *Therefore every loss of revelation is at the same time a loss of language.* When language itself aims to be revelation it loses itself as language.[44] But where revelation commandeers language, *the word of God* takes place. The word of God *brings* language to its true essence.[45]

If in the interpretation of the revelation there is a gain to

---

[43] At this point the hermeneutical interest of theology and its application to the historical-critical method meet each other. The historical-critical method, in that it investigates language (of the text) as language (and not at all as revelation), attempts to get to know the revelation in the language of the text. The historical-critical method thus orientates itself (exclusively!) on the *captures* which revelation *has* made when it *has* come to speech. The hermeneutical task of theology consists in bringing revelation as revelation to speech while operating with the historical-critical method. Hermeneutics interests itself in the *capture* of the language by revelation as it becomes perceptible in the captures (texts!). Hermeneutics attempts so to preserve revelation as revelation and language as language precisely where revelation takes place, i.e. where God comes to speech. Hermeneutics is interested in the texts as the captures of the revelation which has come to speech, because it is interested in the reiteration of the event of the capture of language, which takes place when revelation takes place. The hermeneutical task of theology is therefore the most consistent *essence* of the historical-critical method in theology. And therefore 'the historical-critical method of the interpretation of biblical texts has completed its service when the compulsion to preach results from the text' (Ernst Fuchs, 'Die der Theologie durch die historisch-kritische Methode auferlegte Besinnung', in: *Zur Frage nach dem historischen Jesus* (Tübingen, 1960), p. 226).

By preaching we are therefore to understand the reiteration of the capture of language through revelation. Because it is a question of reiteration, the preacher preaches from biblical *texts*. That this reiteration can happen only in *speech* is at the same time an indication concerning the *essence* of language *as* language (but not, indeed, as revelation). The essence of language as language is that God brings himself to speech by capturing the language. Thus language becomes the free place of meeting. Where this meeting takes place language is brought to its true being. Language is brought to its true being where God brings himself to speech. The essence of language is therefore the *event* of the word 'God' (cf. Thomas Bonhoeffer, *RGG³* VI, Article 'Sprache', esp. p. 280f.), but not the *presence* of the *nomen* 'God'.

[44] Loss to language and gain to language therefore consist not in an increase or decrease of language (*nomina*). The *analogia nominum* is very eloquent. Revelation is no gain to language in that it says everything that language allows to be said, but in that it says something definite. Revelation concerns, so to say, selection.

[45] Language must be captured by revelation in order to be brought to its true essence.

language which itself is grounded in the event of revelation, then we shall now have to inquire after the possibility of this gain to language and also after the possibility of the interpretation of revelation. We have already seen that it is a question of the capability of revelation. Yet in what sense *can* revelation make demands on language? It can do so only because it speaks as revelation itself. 'If we know what revelation is, even in deliberately speaking about it we shall be content to let revelation speak for itself.'[46] The revelation of God thus 'commandeers' language not as a dumb aggressor but enters into language as a movement of speech. The revelation of God is no silent demand for language but by its speaking makes demands on the language. Thus *the revelation of God itself is the enabling of the interpretation of revelation.* It is so, therefore, 'because revelation is the self-interpretation of this God'.[47] But revelation as the *self-interpretation of God* is the root of the doctrine of the Trinity. The doctrine of the Trinity is then consequently the interpretation of revelation and therewith the interpretation of the being of God made possible by revelation as the self-interpretation of God.

A hermeneutic which inquires after the self-interpretation of God is in essence something different from the Aristotelian hermeneutic of signification. That remains valid *in spite of* many responsive chords in Barth's *Church Dogmatics* to this hermeneutic of signification.

(b) Revelation as God's self-interpretation

'Revelation is the Person of God speaking (*Dei loquentis persona*).'[48] When we inquire after the being of God, we shall therefore have to let ourselves be guided by the answer which becomes loud in the revelation, because in God's revelation 'God's word is identical with God himself'.[49] And since in revelation 'the fullness of the original self-existent *being* of God's word'[50] reposes and lives, then revelation is that event in which

---

[46] *CD* I/1, p. 347.   [47] *CD* I/1, p. 311.
[48] *CD* I/1, p. 304.   [49] *CD* I/1, p. 304.   [50] *CD* I/1, p. 305.

the *being of God* itself comes to word.

The being of God, however, for Barth, does not come to speech only as a content of revelation. Revelation is indeed the self-interpretation of God, thus an event that does not let itself be distinguished into form and content. 'The distinction between form and content cannot be applied to the biblical concept of revelation. When revelation is an event according to the Bible, there is no second question as to what its content might be.'[51] Since, however, God reveals himself in the event of revelation we have to do with God both in the *event* (1) of revelation as well as in the revealed *content* (2) of this event. And since God is therefore manifest in revelation because *he* (3) has revealed himself, we have in revelation to do with the being of God in a *threefold* way. When therefore the being of God is recognized in revelation then indeed we know 'that the God who reveals himself in the Bible must also be recognized in his revealing . . . if he is to be recognized at all'.[52] For God 'in unimpaired unity is the revealer, the revelation and the revealedness', or as it may also be put, 'the revealing God *and* the event of revelation *and* its effect on man'.[53] So then, God is subject, predicate and object of the revelation-event. The question what God is may, according to the biblical witness, only be answered when immediately and first of all 'the other two questions as well: What is he doing? and, What does he effect?'[54] are answered. Already in *Die christliche Dogmatik*[55] Barth had thought that the Christian concept of revelation would have to be found in the answer to 'the questions concerning subject, predicate and object of the proposition: "God speaks", "*Deus dixit*" ' and he viewed this concept of revelation as the foundation of the doctrine of the Trinity. In spite of many contradictions which were encountered he held fast to this in the *Church Dogmatics*.

In revelation, therefore, we have to do with *one* internally-

[51] *CD* I/1, p. 306.　　　　[52] *CD* I/1, p. 298.
[53] *CD* I/1, p. 299.　　　　[54] *CD* I/1, p. 297.
[55] *Die christliche Dogmatik im Entwurf. Die Lehre vom Worte Gottes. Prolegomena zur christlichen Dogmatik* (Munich, 1927), p. 127.

distinguished being of God. The *oneness* of this internally-distinguished being of God is grounded in the fact that revelation is 'not an other over against God' but 'a reiteration of God'.[56] In that God *can* reiterate himself, in that he *executes* this reiteration and in that he *has* thus reiterated himself, the internally-distinguished being of God becomes recognizable in its *differentiation*. The doctrine of the Trinity considers the oneness and differentiation of God's being. It considers the 'threefold mode of being'[57] which constitutes its differentiation in the oneness of God's being. In that the doctrine of the Trinity does this, it explicates the statement 'God reveals himself as the Lord'.[58] In just this way the doctrine of the Trinity is the interpretation of God's self-interpretation.

[56] *CD* I/1, p. 299.　　　　　[57] *CD* I/1, p. 299.

[58] *CD* I/1, p. 306. That God reveals himself as the Lord is certainly also looked upon by F. W. J. Schelling as the fundamental proposition of the doctrine of the Trinity when he thinks of 'the three Persons' of the Trinity 'as the three Lords of times which follow one another'. In that Schelling understands the time before the creation as 'the time of the Father in a special sense', the present time 'as the time of the Son in a pre-eminent sense' and the future time 'during the whole creation' as 'the time of the Spirit', the suspicion of Sabellianism which immediately arises does not apply to him, since Schelling recommends that 'these three times in contrast' to 'that merely temporal time which originates namely through the merely constant reiteration of the one world-time = A' should be called '*eternal*' times. 'For with the statement which is often made, that there is no time outside our world or that it is a mere form of our sensuous existence, and the like, one can comprehend nothing of the divine economy of three Persons as it is presented in revelation, nor of the revelation itself. These and similar weak concepts must be rejected in order to penetrate into the great mystery which has been *unlocked and opened up* by Christianity' (Philosophie der Offenbarung. *Sämmtliche Werke II*, 4, Stuttgart and Augsburg, 1858, p. 71f.).

In Schelling's interpretation of the three Persons of the Trinity as 'three Lords of times which follow one another' (which, by the way, rests on an 'exegesis' of 1 Cor. 15. 25), the question concerns an appropriation [the act of attributing a certain attribute or work to one particular Person of the Godhead. See below, pp. 36f – Tr.] which at the same time lays bare the inadequacy of the common concept of time. That the appropriation does not exclude a *perichoresis* [the interpenetration and mutual immanence of the three *hypostases* of the Trinity, as taught by John of Damascus – Tr.] of the 'three successive Lords' (*ibid.* p. 71) is shown by Schelling's statements that it concerns 'the time of the Father' only 'in a special sense' and 'the time of the Son' only 'in a pre-eminent sense'. With regard to 'the time of the Spirit' a corresponding qualifying addition is lacking because 'the glory of

Barth begins – corresponding to the historical development of the doctrine of the Trinity and corresponding to the actual theme of the biblical witness – with the *event* of revelation, with 'God's *action* in his revelation'.[59] Barth's doctrine of the Trinity is already Christologically grounded – not only through the claim that revelation is the root of the doctrine of the Trinity, but beyond this, especially through his beginning with the event of God's manifestation within the three moments to be distinguished in the concept of revelation. The Christological grounding is orientated formally on the concept of God. In his revelation God takes form and reveals himself just as form. God's 'taking form' is 'his self-unveiling'.[60] We shall have to understand God's 'taking form' in the sense of the concept of God's reiteration. For God's 'taking form' is to be so understood, that God 'in his revelation is his own double'.[61] God's taking form is thus not an *accidens* of God 'but an event'[62] and, indeed, an event which presupposes a self-distinction in God, 'something new in God, a self-distinction of God from himself, a being of God in a mode of existence . . . in which he can also exist *for us*'.[63] With this teaching about the self-differentiating of God in his being, Barth is concerned to know that God's revelation is grounded *alone* in God's being and to hold every synergistic thought far from the Christian concept of revelation. That God is for us, that he is not only hidden as he himself for himself, but manifest for us as he who is hidden God for himself – that must be grounded in the being of God. 'The God who reveals himself here *can* reveal himself. The very fact of revelation tells us that it is *proper* to him to distinguish himself from himself, i.e. to be God in himself and in concealment and yet at the same time in a very different way, namely, in

---

the Spirit is added to that of the Father and of the Son' for the 'common glorification of the Father, Son and Spirit' (*ibid.* p. 73).

That Schelling's doctrine of the Trinity is fundamentally different from that of Barth's – in spite of the parallel (and even in it) which we have shown – will remain hidden from no one who does not fail to busy himself with the relevant statements in Schelling's writings.

[59] *CD* I/1, p. 314.   [60] *CD* I/1, p. 316.
[61] *CD* I/1, p. 316.   [62] *CD* I/1, p. 316.   [63] *CD* I/1, p. 316.

manifestation, i.e. to be *God a second time* in the form of some-thing he himself is not':[64] God the Son. 'This Sonship is God's lordship in his revelation.'[65]

According to this starting-point it cannot be doubted that God in 'his first, hidden mode of being' cannot be understood as a God who stands alienated from his revelation. The *deus absconditus* is not a God who is hostile to his revelation. He is rather, precisely as the *deus absconditus*, that is, in his hidden mode of being, the subject of revelation. The fact that this subject of revelation is the God who cannot be unveiled to man, heightens and secures the concept of revelation as God's *self*-unveiling. In his self-unveiling God unveils himself as he who is inscrut-able. 'In saying this we naturally mean that in his *revealed* nature he is thus inscrutable. It is the *Deus revelatus* who is the *Deus absconditus*.'[66] Thus revelation remains God's revelation. The *event* of revelation remains protected from becoming a happening in which God loses himself. As event revelation may only be thought of, in so far as this event is constituted through God's being as subject. '*Revelation* always means *revealing*'; for 'God's presence is always *God's decision to be present*'.[67] The God who *can* reveal himself is not *obliged* to reveal himself. 'God's self-unveiling remains an act of sovereign divine freedom.'[68] Therefore God as the subject of revelation *remains* distinguished from revelation. Were this not so then revelation would cease to be revelation. For it is not '*the form* which reveals, speaks, comforts, works and aids, *but God in the form*'.[69] But precisely in this way God reveals himself 'as the Father of the Son in whom he takes form for our sake' without thereby ceasing to be 'the free ground and the free power of his being God in the Son'.[70]

If revelation as event allows us to perceive God in a mode of being in which he can also be for us, then it will belong to the essence of revelation that this 'being for us' also really comes to its final goal. Moreover, the fact that revelation is '*a concrete*

[64] *CD* I/1, p. 316.   [65] *CD* I/1, p. 320.   [66] *CD* I/1, p. 321.
[67] *CD* I/1, p. 321.   [68] *CD* I/1, p. 321.
[69] *CD* I/1, p. 321.   [70] *CD* I/1, p. 324.

relation to concrete men'[71] must be grounded in the essence of the
revelation itself if 'God's revelation has its reality and truth
wholly and in every respect . . . within itself'.[72] Here also a
consequent resistance against a synergistic concept of revelation
is once more carried on when the subject matter – that revelation is 'the self-unveiling of God *imparted to men*',[73] – is understood as being exclusively grounded in revelation itself. As a
happening imparted to men revelation is an historical event.

'Part of the concept of the biblically attested revelation
is that it is an *historical event.*'[74] With the concept of the 'historicality of revelation' Barth expresses the fact that revelation
takes place factually, is ascertainable (not historically in the
sense of positivism!) and recognizable as an 'event different
from every other event, and which is thus incomparable and
cannot be repeated'.[75] In this sense revelation 'in the Bible is
a matter of impartation, of God's being revealed'.[76] Only
through God's being historically revealed do the two previously
recognized 'relationships, in which the Bible regards God as
existing',[77] remain protected from being myths. 'Without God's
being historically revealed in this way, revelation would not be
revelation. God's being revealed makes it a *link* between God
and man, an effective encounter between God and man. But
it is God's own being revealed that makes it this.'[78] Here also
it is a question of the *being* of God, of a mode of being peculiar
to himself. This moment of revelation, too, is itself grounded in
the being of God. And this grounding of revelation in the
being of the God who reveals himself becomes intelligible
through the revelation itself. In the 'self-disclosing unity of
the Father and the Son which discloses itself to men',[79] God
can 'do what the biblical witnesses ascribe to him, namely, not
just take form and not just *remain free* in this form, but also in this
form and freedom of his *become God to specific men*, eternity in a

[71] *CD* I/1, p. 325.   [72] *CD* I/1, p. 305.
[73] *CD* I/1, p. 324.   [74] *CD* I/1, p. 325.
[75] *CD* I/1, p. 329.   [76] *CD* I/1, p. 330.
[77] *CD* I/1, p. 330.   [78] *CD* I/1, p. 331.
[79] *CD* I/1, p. 332.

moment'.[80] This is meant when it is said that 'God reveals himself as the *Spirit*'.[81]

God reveals himself as the Lord. That, for Barth, is the basic axiom of revelation. We saw what that means. If revelation is the self-interpretation of God, then in revelation God interprets himself *as* the one who he *is*. Thus in the event of this self-interpretation he reveals himself as revealer, as revelation and as revealedness. But in these capacities God reveals himself at the same time as he who *can* reveal himself, i.e. as the Lord. The concept of the lordship of God is for Barth the expression of the capability of revelation and thus of the possibility of revelation, which is grounded in the being of God. This possibility of being able to reveal himself does not, however, exist apart from the capacities in which God 're-iterates' himself. The proposition which underlies Barth's ontology: 'Where the actuality exists there is also the corresponding possibility',[82] is also true here. If God is able to reveal himself then he must reveal himself as the *Lord* in *all* as-relationships. If he reveals himself as he who he is, if his interpretation of himself is complete, then the *being* of God which becomes thematic in the capacities of revelation must correspond to his 'function' observed in the self-interpretation as revealer, revelation and revealedness.[83] Therefore the dogma of the Trinity is the appropriate expression for God's being. It protects the Christian doctrine of God from becoming mythological[84] or slipping into metaphysics.[85]

Precisely this critical-polemical function of Barth's doctrine of the Trinity has not been adequately considered. Paradoxical

---

[80] *CD* I/1, p. 331.   [81] *CD* I/1, p. 332.   [82] *CD* II/1, p. 5.

[83] In Barth's writings this view works itself out formally in that within the Trinitarian sections concerning God the Father, God the Son and God the Holy Spirit, in each case God is first treated with respect to the 'function in revelation' which he has as creator, reconciler and redeemer and then in each case in his mode of being as eternal Father, eternal Son and eternal Spirit.

[84] *CD* I/1, p. 327.

[85] In Greek thought both lie very close to each other, cf. Aristotle, *Metaphysics* A, 982 b 18 f.: . . . 'Even the lover of myth is in a sense a lover of wisdom' (ὁ φιλόμυθος φιλόσοφός πώς ἐστιν).

as it may sound, the doctrine of the Trinity in Barth's theology (1932) has the same function as the programme of demythologizing in the theology of Rudolf Bultmann. The difference of methods and results here and there is not able to obscure this. This fact should give cause for reflection to the over-hasty and superficial critics of Bultmann, and the critics of Barth who are constantly ready and pleased to reproach the *Church Dogmatics* with the charge of speculation[86] while they themselves are less willing and pleased to read Barth's writings. If we understand Bultmann's programme as the concern for appropriate speech about God (and therewith about man) and if we view the fulfilment of this concern as a concern not to objectify God or let him be objectified as an It or He, but to bring him to speech as Thou and thus to speak of him appropriately, then we shall not fail to recognize a conspicuous parallelism to the significance which Barth attributes (and gives) to the doctrine of the Trinity. For the significance – not the final, but certainly a primary significance – of the doctrine of the Trinity for Barth consists in ensuring over against subordinationism on the one hand and modalism on the other, that God becomes 'neither an It nor a He': 'he remains Thou'.[87] While subordinationism rests upon the intention of making out of the God who reveals himself 'the kind of subject . . . which we can survey, grasp and master, which can be objectified',[88] the doctrine of the Trinity, according to Barth, has precisely the task of comprehending the 'subject of revelation' as '*the*

---

[86] The reproach of speculation against theologians who think consistently is old. The accusation of Bernard of Clairvaux against Peter Abelard is an instructive example. 'This man disputes about the faith against the faith; he sees nothing mysterious and as in a mirror dimly, but he understands everything from face to face. He wants to go beyond his limitations. Of everything in heaven and on earth he maintains that nothing is unknown to him except he himself. He pushes back the boundaries which our fathers accepted in that he brings the most lofty questions about revelation to discussion. To his pupils, who are as yet completely inexperienced, scarcely educated, scarcely weaned from dialectic, scarcely capable of comprehending the basic truths of the faith, he opens up the mystery of the Trinity, the most holy place and the private chamber of the King' (cited by Martin Grabmann, *Die Geschichte der scholastischen Methode*, 2nd ed.; Berlin, 1956, II, p. 171f.).   [87] *CD* I/1, p. 381.   [88] *CD* I/1, p. 381.

subject' that 'remains *indissolubly* subject'.[89] And while modalism seeks the actual God beyond the three moments of revelation in a higher being in which are no distinctions, and thus allows the Thou of God to disappear and an 'objectifying'[90] of God to appear in its place, the doctrine of the Trinity, according to Barth, has the task of preventing the 'revelation of God and thus his being' . . . from becoming 'an economy which is foreign to his essence'.[91] Correspondingly, it is the express purpose of the doctrine of the Trinity, a purpose which it is the doctrine's task vehemently to defend, to make clear that, and how far, the God who reveals himself can be (*a*) 'our *God*' and (*b*) '*our* God'.[92] He can be (*a*) 'our *God*, because in all his modes of being he is equal to himself, one and the same Lord'. And as this Lord he can be (*b*) '*our* God. He can meet us and unite himself to us, because he is God in his three modes of being as Father, Son and Spirit, because creation, reconciliation and redemption, the whole being, speech and action in which he wills to be our God, have their basis and prototype in his own essence, in his own being as God.'[93]

The 'whole being, speech and action' in which God wills to be *our* God is, for Barth, revelation. 'According to the Bible God's being with us is the event of revelation.'[94] It was held valid for this revelation that it has 'its reality and truth wholly and in every respect . . . within itself'.[95] When it is now said of this revelation of God that it has 'its basis and prototype in his own essence, in his own being as God',[96] then this basis and prototype in the essence and being of God himself must also belong to its reality and truth. That means, however, that God's being *ad extra corresponds* essentially to his being *ad intra* in which it has its basis and prototype. God's *self*-interpretation (revelation) is interpretation as correspondence. Let it be well noted: *as* his own *interpreter* God corresponds to his own being. Since, however, God as his own interpreter (also in his external works) *is* he himself, since also in this happening as such it is

---

[89] *CD* I/1, p. 382.   [90] *CD* I/1, p. 382.   [91] *CD* I/1, p. 382.
[92] *CD* I/1, p. 383.   [93] *CD* I/1, p. 383.   [94] *CD* I/1, p. 307.
[95] *CD* I/1, p. 305.   [96] *CD* I/1, p. 383f.

a question of the *being* of God, then the highest and last statement which can be made about the being of God is:

God corresponds to himself.[97]

In actuality Barth's *Dogmatics* is basically a detailed exegesis of this proposition. When this proposition is not understood as an attempt to objectify God, but as an attempt to comprehend the mystery of God there where it becomes manifest as a mystery, then it implies a *movement* which above and beyond genius and diligence makes possible a dogmatics of the calibre of the *Church Dogmatics*. The *Church Dogmatics* is the ingenious and diligent attempt to think the proposition 'God corresponds to himself' through to the end.

Before we proceed to Barth's doctrine of God in the narrower sense by means of this leading proposition for the interpretation of God's being, we have still to show the consequences of this proposition for the doctrine of the Trinity. We may now start out from the point that in the doctrine of the Trinity the question concerns the being of the God who reveals himself in the sense of the ability to be. Thus the doctrine of the Trinity tells us 'that the God who reveals himself according to Scripture is both to be feared and also to be loved, to be *feared* because he can be God and to be *loved* because he can be our God. That he *is* these two things the doctrine of the Trinity as such cannot tell us.'[98] Here the doctrine of the Trinity points back to Scripture and to the revelation of God himself which is witnessed to in it; the doctrine of the Trinity is meant to be the interpretation of this revelation. The doctrine of the Trinity, therefore, does not take the place of revelation, because no statements can take the place of the event of the word of God itself. 'No dogma and no theology as such can do that.'[99] The doctrine of the Trinity intends to effectuate everything save human constructions. If it wanted to effectuate human constructions it would lead itself *ad absurdum*. For it would then

---

[97] Cf. *CD* II/1, pp. 657 and 660; there the 'form of the perfect being of God' is defined as the 'wonderful unity of identity and non-identity, of simplicity and multiplicity, inward and outward'.
[98] *CD* I/1, p. 383.   [99] *CD* I/1, p. 383.

cease to be the interpretation of an event.

The doctrine of the Trinity, according to Barth, should rather prevent the being of God being understood as a human construction. In that it teaches us that God as 'Father, Son and Spirit . . . is, so to speak, ours in advance',[100] it will call our attention to the fact that God as the God already ours in advance is completely his own, that he who 'posits himself in the hiddenness of his Godhead is his own origin'.[101]

(c) The self-relatedness of God's being (in the distinction of the three modes of God's being)

That God corresponds to himself is an expression of a relationship. With respect to the being of God this proposition signifies that this being is a being structured as a relationship. The relational structuring of God's being showed itself in the phenomenon of revelation, which as such is also structured as a relation, and just in this its relational structuring expresses the relational structure of God's being. The concept of structure is certainly open to misunderstanding in so far as it can be understood in the sense of immovability. The question of the relations within God's being which have been brought to expression through revelation, however, concerns 'genetic relations'[102] by which God's being is differentiated into different modes of being.

With the concept of the mode of being Barth takes up the Patristic term 'mode of subsistence' (τρόπος ὑπάρξεως) in order to replace the misleading concept of Person. The oneness of God's being is differentiated in that three different modes of being are distinguished. The differentiation between these three modes of being is to be understood from the relationships which hold them together. Those particular features of the modes of God's being which are given to one another through the mutual relations within the modes of being constitute the modes of God's being as 'modes of being'.[103] Only as modes of

[100] CD I/1, p. 383.   [101] CD I/1, p. 372.
[102] CD I/1, p. 363.   [103] CD I/1, p. 363.

being distinguished from one another through their mutual relations and *formally* marked out by their respective particular features, can one derive the 'Trinity in unity' of God's being from the concept of revelation. Only in the sense of an *analogia relationis* and *attributionis extrinsecae* do the modes of God's being, revealed in their (economic-Trinitarian) reality correspond to the revelation of their (immanent-Trinitarian) capacity. According to Barth there is no possibility of deriving the difference in the three modes of being from the material differences in the thought of God contained in the concept of revelation.[104] An *analogia attributionis intrinsecae* according to which the modes of God's being reiterate their substantial content in revelation, does not come into question. For the 'relatively differentiated revelation of the three modes of being does not imply a corresponding differentiation among themselves'.[105] The oneness of God's being must be shown precisely in the differentiation of the three modes of being among themselves.[106] The critical canon of the relation between the differentiation of the modes of being and their 'oneness in this distinction'[107] is the 'Trinitarian-theological axiom: *opera trinitatis ad extra sunt indivisa*'.[108]

The disregarding of this axiom and the assertion of an analogy with respect to content between the relatively differentiated becoming revealed of the three modes of God's being and their differentiation in themselves would in the final analysis mean that the becoming revealed of the being of God is *impossible*. However certain it is that revelation as the self-interpretation of God is also the self-identification of God, it is equally certain that there is no *identity* separable from the *event* of self-identification between the being of God and a being understood (but then only incorrectly) as revelation,[109]

---

[104] *CD* I/1, p. 363.

[105] *CD* I/1, p. 362.

[106] From this point objections against Barth's teaching concerning 'God's passion' and the reproach of the threatening tritheism are carefully dedended; see below, pp. 83f.

[107] *CD* I/1, p. 362.

[108] *CD* I/1, pp. 362 and 375.   [109] *CD* I/1, p. 326,

a being in which the *alius, alius, alius* of the Trinity would be perverted into an *aliud, aliud, aliud.* If revelation, however, is understood as the *event* of God's self-identification, then with the oneness of the distinctions between revealer, becoming revealed and being revealed which constitutes this event, revelation enables that very relation-analogy which allows us to distinguish the being of God into three modes of being in the sense of different genetic relationships to one another. Just as the revelation is to be distinguished into (*a*) a whence of revelation, (*b*) a becoming revealed which is grounded in this whence, and (*c*) a being revealed of God which is grounded in the whence *and* in the becoming revealed, so 'in the essence or act in which God is God there are first a pure origin and then two different issues (*Ausgänge*)' to be distinguished, 'the first of which is to be attributed solely to the origin and the second and different one to both the origin and also the first issue. . . . God is . . . God in the very mode or way that he is in those relationships to himself.'[110]

The being of God is thus a being differentiated in itself and thus related in its distinctions, whereby the relationship constitutes the distinction. But that means that these very relationships are not impersonal structural elements in God but that God's being as being is pure *event*. It is a question of a 'reiteration in God', a '*repetitio aeternitatis in aeternitate* by which the oneness of the revealed God is differentiated from everything else that may be called oneness'.[111] Therefore this being is to be grounded by nothing apart from itself and, indeed, without thereby wanting to claim for itself the metaphysical title of a *summum ens.* The conferring of this title would rather rob the divine being as event of its priority which is grounded in itself, because it would be able to comprehend God *only* as an elevation of experienced being. To confer such a title would be to misunderstand that '*alius-alius-alius* . . . does not mean *aliud-alius-aliud*', that the ontological unanimity of oneness and differentiation in God's being knows 'no analogies' because this ontological unanimity is 'the singular (!) divine threeness

---

[110] *CD* I/1, p. 364.   [111] *CD* I/1, p. 366.

D

in the singular (!) divine oneness'.[112] The singularity of this being of God as event would then be already surrendered if within the possible relations between the three modes of God's being one wanted to postulate a fourth independent mode of divine being apart from the being of the Father (in virtue of which 'God the Father is the Father of the Son'), the being of the Son (in virtue of which 'God the Son is the Son of the Father') and the being of the Spirit (in virtue of which 'God the Spirit is the Spirit of the Father and the Son') – namely the 'fourth logically possible and actual relation, the active relation of the Father and the Son to the Spirit'.[113] Being as event is only to be comprehended in its divine singularity as 'threehood' (*Gedritt*)[114] not as 'fourhood' (*Geviert*).[115] In 'fourhood' the philosopher seeks to think of the being as event. He has then deliberately renounced the intention to think through the singularity of God. This renunciation deserves theological respect in so far as it has basically said farewell to the attempt to confer titles on God (an attempt, perhaps, to protect the singularity of God in that it is not thought but does not remain unconsidered?). A singular revelation, also, or better, revelation in its singularity, can certainly no longer be thought of. On the contrary, revelation becomes a fundamental determinant of all that exists in so far as this shows itself originally as itself. Over against this we shall have to remember that God is so to speak 'ours in advance' precisely in his being as 'threehood', as 'Father, Son and Spirit'.[116] If God in his being as threehood is already ours in advance, then this singular being in the freedom of his being-as-event *is* love. But singular love is the being of God precisely as threehood. The self-giving in which God is already ours *in advance* is the self-giving in which *he* belongs *to himself*. This self-giving is the self-relatedness of God's being within the modes of being of the Father, the Son

---

[112] *CD* I/1, p. 364.   [113] *CD* I/1, p. 365.
[114] Concept from M. Luther, WA 46, p. 436 and WA 49, p. 238f.
[115] Concept from M. Heidegger; cf. e.g. 'Bauen Wohnen Denken', in: *Vorträge und Aufsätze* (Pfullingen, 1954) p. 145f. The rejection of a divine 'fourhood' was expressly pronounced by the 4th Lateran Council: '*in Deo* TRINITAS *est solummodo* NON QUATERNITAS.'   [116] *CD* I/1, p. 383.

and the Spirit, which must be differentiated. In the self-relatedness of God's being the relational structuring of this being *eventuates*.[117] As the mutual self-giving of the three modes of God's being, the being of God is event. Because the being of God as threehood is self-giving (love), this being may not be thought of as something abstract. Where it becomes abstract it is not comprehended as God's being. For 'being is actually something abstract only where it is abstracted from love'.[118] The self-relatedness of God's being signifies that God is Lord of himself. That distinguishes him from man. For the self-relatedness of man as *homo incurvatus in se* signifies that man is not lord of himself (Rom. 1. 18f.).

(*d*) *The concreteness of God's being* (perichoresis *and appropriation of the three modes of God's being*)

We have maintained that Barth's doctrine of the Trinity as dogmatic interpretation of God's self-interpretation possesses an anti-metaphysical and anti-mythological significance. It has this significance in so far as it teaches us to think of God's

[117] What H. Gollwitzer rejects for the relationship between God's being and man when he criticizes the statement that God's being is 'only the event of this relation' (*The Existence of God*, p. 50) is true, according to Barth, precisely for the being of God in his self-relatedness. The being of God *eventuates* in the mutual relations of the modes of God's being and is actually identical with this event. But when God in this his being as threehood is already ours in advance, then the reservations of Bultmann and his pupils against that objectification of God must actually find a great deal of understanding which I cannot discover in the book of G. Noller cited by Gollwitzer (*op. cit.* p. 50, fn. 1) (cf. *Sein und Existenz. Die Überwindung des Subjekt-Objekt-Schemas in der Philosophie Heideggers und in der Theologie der Entmythologisierung*, Munich, 1962). Why then does one prefer the most extremely questionable interpretations of Bultmann to one's own interpretation of Bultmann '*in bonam partem*'? That Gollwitzer concerns himself about his own interpretation of Bultmann '*in bonam partem*' shall in no way be disputed, but be acknowledged with satisfaction. Nevertheless it is still misleading when one states all the possible dangerous consequences of Bultmann's theology but simply repeats what Noller advances against Bultmann instead of advancing what Bultmann says and intends against such a questionable interpretation as that of Noller's (for a criticism of Noller cf. *EvTh* 1963, p. 218f.).

[118] Thomas Bonhoeffer, *Die Gotteslehre des Thomas von Aquin*, p. 41.

being as event and thus enables us to think of God as the God who reveals himself. Barth's doctrine of the Trinity attempts to formulate the being of God as event, in that it formulates the being of God as distinguished being, as being differentiated within itself. This, on the other hand, takes place in that the different modes of God's being in which and as which God is God, are differentiated. The three modes of God's being as Father, Son and Spirit are to be thought of as differentiated from one another in the same measure as they are to be thought of as related to one another.[119] The mutual relations of the three divine modes of being are to be thought of as the self-relatedness of the divine being. In this self-relatedness the being of God is understood as *event*. The self-relatedness of God's being makes possible the self-interpretation of God. God *reveals* himself *as* Father, Son and Spirit because he *is* God *as* Father, Son and Spirit. As the mutual self-giving of the divine modes of being, the self-relatedness of God's being is the enabling and in so far the anticipated reflection of God's self-giving in which he is ours. If we are enabled to formulate this self-giving of God in which he is ours as concrete event, then we must also formulate the being of God in the event of the self-relatedness of this being as *concrete* being. For the assertion that God's being in his self-relatedness is to be thought of as event would remain empty if it were not intelligible to what extent the being of God is concrete event. It must, then, be

[119] Ludwig Feuerbach perceived that extremely well: 'The divine Persons distinguish themselves . . . from one another only where they relate themselves reciprocally to one another.' Feuerbach, however, draws the conclusion that God's being in the dogma of the Trinity is thought of not as concrete being but as completely abstract being, because 'Person . . . here is only a relative concept, the concept of a relation.' There is here, certainly, a confusion of personality and person when Feuerbach – in the ostensible distinction to human being – maintains with respect to the being of the divine 'Persons' that 'only the abstract Fatherhood grounds its personality, its distinction from the Son, whose personality likewise grounds only the abstract Sonship'. Cf. *The Essence of Christianity*, Harper Torchbook, 1957, pp. 232–5. Barth brought the Trinitarian dogma with the directly opposite conclusions, doubtless with more originality, or let us say, biblically, to its true worth, when he understood the dogma as the attempt to formulate God's being concretely.

made intelligible to what extent the unity of the three modes
of God's being is a *concrete* oneness and to what extent the
differentiation of the three modes of being remains a *concrete*
differentiation precisely in this concrete oneness. Thinking
which concerns itself about such intelligibility must necessarily
become more difficult and 'abstract' in order to be able to
formulate the concreteness of God's being. That may be vexing;
it should, however, suggest a certain caution to those theologians who are of the opinion that the problems raised by
H. Braun, for example, are easily settled when one as frequently
and as loudly as possible assures everyone that God is concrete,
objective and able to be treated as an object, etc. (It belongs
to the merit of H. Gollwitzer with his book on the 'existence
of God' to have drawn our attention to the difficulty of the
problem which must be treated.) So obvious as it may appear
that God's being in his self-relatedness is to be formulated as
concrete being, the mastering of this problem of formulation is
still extremely difficult.[120]

In Barth's doctrine of the Trinity the doctrine of *perichoresis*
and the doctrine of appropriation serve to master this difficulty.
The concreteness of God's being will be formulated with the
help of these doctrines. After the foregoing discussion it does
not require to be especially emphasized any further that in this
task of formulation it is not a question of the postulates of
formulation. On the contrary, it is a question of grappling with
the systematic problems which theology has been set by the
revelation which has taken place.

In the *being* revealed of God, the being of God for Barth is
concrete as historical event. In this concreteness the self-
communication of God takes place. In God's self-communication there comes about also his fellowship with man. But in

[120] 'Did not one of the most famous theologians at the beginning of the
last century [i.e. the 18th century], Christoph Matthäus Pfaff, who lacked
neither learning nor the endeavour to be orthodox, make the frank admis-
sion that in the doctrine of the Trinity he could well understand each
moment taken separately, but that it was impossible for him to fit the whole
with all moments and determinations into his head?' (Schelling, *op. cit.*
p. 66f.).

this self-communication of God to man *all* three divine modes
of being are at work according to the Trinitarian-theological
axiom *'opera trinitatis ad extra sunt indivisa'*. If the concreteness
of God's self-communication to man is to be thoroughly
comprehended, then the self-relatedness of God's being in the
differentiation of the three modes of being must likewise be
comprehended as fellowship in which the being of God takes
place concretely. This fellowship is given through 'a complete
participation of each mode of being in the other modes of
being'.[121] Through this reciprocal participation the three modes
of being *become* concretely united. In this concrete unity they
are God. Becoming and being are here originally together
because the concrete[122] unity of God's being is 'the oneness of
being one, which is always also a *becoming* one'.[123] None of the
divine modes of being, then, exists in abstraction from the
others. Even the mutual *relatedness* of the modes of being is no
abstract structuring of the being of God. But the mutual relatedness of the modes of being *takes place* as participation in
each other, as *circumincessio*,[124] as περιχώρησις. In this participa-

---

[121] *CD* I/1, p. 370.

[122] According to Hegel 'concrete' is derived from *'concrescere'* [to grow
together], so that for the designation of this subject matter there could be
no better word. Hegel sought in this way to think of God as concrete being.
Cf. for example his *Aesthetik* (new ed., Berlin, 1955), p. 108f.; ET (4 vols.,
London, 1920), p. 86f. 'When we say, for example, of God that he is simply
One, the Supreme Being as such, we have merely expressed a lifeless
abstraction of irrational understanding. Such a God who is not conceived
in his concrete truth will be unable to provide any content for art, especially
sculpture and painting. Thus neither the Jews nor the Turks have been able
to represent their God, who is never simply such an abstraction of the
understanding, through art in the positive way in which Christians have
represented him. For in Christianity God is represented in his truth and
therefore as thoroughly concrete in himself, as person, as subject and more
accurately as spirit. And what he is as spirit becomes more explicit for the
religious conception as a Trinity of persons which at the same time is
implicitly one person. Here is essentiality, universality and particularity no
less than their reconciled unity, and only such a unity is concrete unity.'

[123] *CD* I/1, p. 369.

[124] Because the relatedness of the modes of being *takes place* as participation
in one another, the other term which is used in Latin writings for the
designation of this subject matter, *circuminsessio*, is less to be recommended.

tion it is a question of a 'passing into one another', through which a trespass of one mode of being against another is impossible.[125] Rather does the *perichoresis* work 'that the divine modes of being mutually condition and permeate one another so completely that one is always in the other two and the other two in the one'.[126] The doctrine of *perichoresis* helps us to formulate the concrete unity of the being of God in that we think of the modes of God's being as meeting one another in unrestricted participation.

Over against the possible objection that with such theological statements about a happening which is not directly related to men a metaphysics is now encouraged which, in a Platonic way, divides up reality into two 'worlds' in one of which God exists 'for himself' and in the other of which God exists 'for us', it is to be remembered that in all his Trinitarian statements Barth is concerned about the oneness of the reality of *God*. 'God's essence and work are not twofold but one.'[127] Yet Barth distinguishes strictly between the reality of God and the reality which owes its existence to God's work. But because for Barth God's work and essence are not of two different kinds, it is for him impossible that the reality of God and the reality which owes its existence to God's work should be related to each other as two different ontological strata and even less that they should fall apart as two worlds separated through a χωρισμός (division). If one wanted to let the reality of God 'be tacked on to earthly reality as an additional reality',[128] then all talk of God could then be only supplementary and therefore super-fluous talk. And it would then be again time to remember Schleiermacher's criticism: 'But whoever makes a distinction between this and that world deludes himself.'[129]

[125] Cf. *CD* IV/1, p. 203.   [126] *CD* I/1, p. 370.   [127] *CD* I/1, p. 371.
[128] Gerhard Ebeling, *Wort und Glaube* (Tübingen, 1962), p. 432; ET, *Word and Faith* (London, 1963), p. 410.
[129] F. Schleiermacher, *Über die Religion, Reden an die Gebildeten unter ihren Verächtern* (3rd ed.; Berlin, 1821), p. 23; cf. the English translation by John Oman, *On Religion. Speeches to its Cultured Despisers* (New York, 1958), p. 20. Karl Barth took thorough account of the significance of this statement of Schleiermacher in his teaching concerning the *eternal* election of the *man*

The reality of God of which Barth speaks is certainly understood falsely when as 'that world' it is set over against another,
namely 'this world'. It is, however, something different to
think of God as God. Nothing else is meant when Barth speaks
of a 'reality of God'. God as God is, however, God in his
essence and work. 'The work of God is the essence of God as
the essence of him who . . . is revealer, revelation and being
revealed, or creator, reconciler and redeemer.'[130]

Barth certainly distinguishes the 'essence of the God who
works and reveals himself' from the 'essence of God as such',[131]

Jesus. What is decisive, certainly, is where a 'distinction . . . between this and
that world' is to come from. For on this 'where' there also rests the decision
whether God appears *on* the horizon of the world or whether the world has
its place *in* the horizon of God.

In that we cite this statement of Schleiermacher as a critical reminder, we
demarcate a boundary between ourselves and H. Gollwitzer, who raises
objection to G. Ebeling's 'rejection of the idea of a God "distinct from the
world" ': 'Whoever . . . only indulges in polemic in the same direction as
Schleiermacher, without also distinguishing himself from him, is omitting
something which is indispensable in a post-Schleiermacher age: the positive
definition of the true, irresolvable and fundamental difference, beyondness
and hence (sic!) objectivity of the God of the Christian proclamation as
compared with man and the world' (*The Existence of God*, p. 177). G. Ebeling's concern, to formulate God not as an extramundane being which can
then still be thought of in a worldly manner as being tacked on to this world,
is indeed, in its way, the attempt to formulate God's being as concrete being.
That Ebeling is concerned (in the school of Luther!) precisely about the
correct distinction between God and man and thus (!) between God and
the world, has been constantly emphasized by him. Cf. for example, 'The
Necessity of the Doctrine of the Two Kingdoms' in *Word and Faith*, p. 403f.,
where it speaks of the man who stands 'truly *coram Deo*' and therefore 'truly
coram mundo. For he knows how to distinguish between what he has to
expect from God and what he has to expect from the world; between what
he has to thank God for and what he has to thank the world for; between
what he owes to God and what he owes to the world. He knows how to
distinguish between God and the world.' And also Ebeling's assertion that
the 'decisive differentiation of reality' is summed up 'solely by the alternative of a believing or unbelieving relation to reality' ('Theology and
Reality', in *Word and Faith*, p. 200) can in no way be misunderstood in a
subjective manner, somehow in the sense that God's being is 'dissolved' into
the subjectivity of faith (a favourite word in the polemic against thinking
theologians), when one considers that Ebeling has defined the essence of
faith as 'participation in the essence of God' ('Jesus and Faith', in *Word and
Faith*, p. 242).   [130] *CD* I/1, p. 371.   [131] *CD* I/1, p. 371.

but this distinction has no other purpose than to establish that
God reveals himself 'not constrained by his essence' but 'in his
free decision'.[132] And correspondingly the assertion that 'God's
work is his essence in its relation to the reality which is distinct
from him and which is to be created or is created',[133] has the
purpose of asserting the concrete oneness of God's being as
the One who reveals himself and as the One who possesses the
capacity of revelation. The capacity of God to reveal himself
(or the essence of God as such, or the being of God in itself) is,
however, not to be understood as another world which man is
able to discover outside of his own. Rather, it concerns the
attempt to express God's being appropriately and, indeed, in
such a way that God's being revealed, which is indeed the
main basis for speech about God's being, is really comprehended as the being revealed *of God*. In order to be able to
speak appropriately of God's work we must talk about the
essence of the One who works. But the essence of this One who
works is now formulated strictly from the point of view of
revelation, thus not as substance, but as the 'unity of Father,
Son and Spirit *among themselves*' to which 'their unity *ad extra*'[134]
corresponds. The significance of the doctrine of *perichoresis* is
that it helps us to formulate this unity of the modes of God's
being among themselves as the concreteness of God's being. It
is the attempt at responsible speech about God.

The concreteness of God's being must now, however, at the
same time be thought of in a counter-movement which – not in
order to make the revelation superfluous, but to be instructed
by it – from the mutual relation of the three modes of God's
being makes the corresponding relation between the unity of
these modes of God's being *among themselves* and their external
unity intelligible. The question thus concerns the *grounding* of
the Trinitarian-theological axiom '*opera trinitatis ad extra sunt
indivisa*'. Such a grounding faces the difficulty of being able to
understand the being of the one God only from his works as
revealer, revelation and being revealed and thus in the differentiation of the three modes of God's being as it becomes

[132] *CD* I/1, p. 371.   [133] *CD* I/1, p. 371.   [134] *CD* I/1, p. 371.

explicit in the differentiation of the works of creation, reconciliation and redemption. At the same time, however, the unity of the modes of God's being must become intelligible in their working; for otherwise 'we should be plunged at once into the error of tritheism'.[135] The difficulty which exists here may be summed up in the question: How is the unity of the divine modes of being able to express itself in God's *work* without surrendering its differentiation? It is thus a question of the oneness of the unity and differentiation of the divine modes of being in the work of God.

'In the vocabulary of the older dogmatics'[136] this problem was considered under the name of the doctrine of appropriations. Appropriation (attribution, assignment) is that act which attributes certain logical predicates to each of the three particular modes of God's being respectively. Barth cites[137] in agreement the definition given by Thomas Aquinas: To appropriate is nothing other than to assign to one person what is common to all (*appropriare nihil est aliud quam commune trahere ad proprium*) and, indeed, so that what is common (*commune*) which has greater resemblance to that which is proper to one Person than with what is proper to the other Person (*maiorem habet similitudinem ad id quod est proprium personae unius quam cum proprio alterius*), is in each case appropriated to this one Person. '*Per appropriationem* this act or this attribute must now be given prominence in relation to this or that mode of being in order that this can be described as such.'[138] Appropriation is thus a hermeneutical procedure for describing the being of God. Thereby particular attributes and operations of the Trinity (in the unity of its modes of being) are respectively ascribed to one particular mode of being. Appropriation, however, *in no way* excludes the attributes and acts ascribed to one particular mode of being from the other modes of being. For appropriation may in no case accompany 'the forgetfulness or denial of God's presence in all his modes of being, in his total being and

---

[135] *CD* I/1, p. 373.   [136] *CD* I/1, p. 373.
[137] *CD* I/1, p. 373; citation from Thomas Aquinas, *De veritate*, qu. 7, art. 3.   [138] *CD* I/1, p. 375.

act'.[139] 'The very knowledge of the intratrinitarian *particularity* guarantees . . . the knowledge of the *oneness* of God.'[140] The unity of the three modes of being has thus to prove itself precisely as *concrete* unity in that *per appropriationem* each of the three modes of being is articulated as itself. Otherwise formulated: the *unity* of the three modes of God's being proves itself as *concrete* unity when it preserves the differentiation of the three modes of being as *concrete* differentiation. In that this takes place the concrete unity articulates itself in oneness with the concrete differentiation of the modes of God's being to form *unanimity as the concreteness* of God's being. In this harmony as the concreteness of God's being is grounded the fact that God in the oneness of unity and differentiation of his modes of being not only *is* but also *expresses himself*: 'to the involution and convolution of the three modes of being in the *essence* of God there corresponds exactly their involution and convolution in his work'.[141]

We called appropriation a hermeneutical procedure. It is this in so far as it happens *per appropriationem* that a mode of God's being 'can be described as such'.[142] Appropriation is thus the possibility of describing God in terms of, e.g., his Fatherhood. We also have appropriation 'before us when in *Luther's Catechism* the concepts of Father and creation, Son and redemption, and Holy Spirit and sanctification are brought into the well-known close relationship to one another'.[143] In the doctrine of appropriations Barth is concerned with the recognition of the 'analogies' to the divine modes of being '*set up in the world*[144] by revelation'.[145] Theological tradition and Barth, too, appear to have understood appropriation as a hermeneutical procedure in the sense that it concerns an act of description by the theologian of the respective *persona trinitatis*. The theologian appropriates. In Barth, though, the usage of

---

[139] *CD* I/1, p. 375.   [140] *CD* I/1, p. 395.   [141] *CD* I/1, p. 374.
[142] *CD* I/1, p. 375.   [145] *CD* I/1, p. 373.
[144] As analogies set up through revelation they are to be strictly distinguished from the *vestigia trinitatis* which are supposed to be 'present in the world' (cf. *CD* I/1, p. 372).   [145] *CD* I/1, p. 372.

language varies. '*Augustine* . . . appropriated . . .';[146] but
Bonaventure has a 'wealth of appropriations which he . . .
partly indicated himself'.[147] What are shown are appropriations
already completed. But who then appropriated?

Barth formulates a decisive axiom of Protestant dogmatics
for the doctrine of appropriation: 'Appropriations must not be
invented freely. They are authentic when they are taken literally
or materially or both from Holy Scripture, when they are a
rendering or interpretation of the appropriations already
found there.'[148] Appropriation as a hermeneutical procedure of
the theologian is thus a follow-up to the act of appropriation
which has already taken place and been completed in Scripture.
And since Scripture testifies to revelation we shall have to
understand revelation itself as the hermeneutical procedure in
which appropriations have their *ratio cognoscendi*. In this sense
Barth speaks of analogies '*set up in the world by* revelation'.[149]

Since for Barth, however, revelation is God's interpretation
of himself, appropriations have their *ratio essendi* in the fellowship which articulates its differentiation of the divine modes of
being themselves. Attribution is that procedure in which God
in the concrete harmony of his modes of being assigns to
himself his being *as Father*, *as Son* and *as Spirit*. Appropriation
is attribution in so far as God assigns to himself his being as the
triune God. In this way God corresponds to himself. Appropriation may therefore not be understood as a supplementary

---

[146] Cf. *CD* I/1, p. 395. In the original the 'appropriation' which we make
is set in inverted commas. Barth says of this appropriation it is 'not just
permitted; it is also commanded', that it is, however, ' "only" an appropriation'. Nevertheless, it corresponds 'with the reality of the revelation
attested to us in Scripture', and certainly 'the impropriety of the knowledge
based upon the appropriation corresponds to the reality of the faith which
apprehends the revelation, which is not sight'. Appropriation here is
doubtless a hermeneutical act of signification (whose subject is man,
certainly as *per analogiam fidei significans*).

[147] *CD* I/1, p. 428. For the anthropological relevance of the Trinitarian
appropriations in scholastic theology we may refer to the excursus on
'Elemente der mittelalterlichen imago-Lehre' in the very instructive book
by Reinhard Schwarz, *Fides, spes und caritas beim jungen Luther. Unter besonderer
Berücksichtigung der mittelalterlichen Tradition* (Berlin, 1962), p. 414f.

[148] *CD* I/1, p. 373.   [149] *CD* I/1, p. 372.

happening which is added to the distinction between the original-relationships in God. Appropriation is a supplementary procedure only in so far as the theologian *per appropriationem* undertakes to describe the individual modes of being of God as such. But this procedure of description must correspond to just that event which articulates the distinction of the original-relationships in the differentiation of the modes of God's being, in that God assigns to himself his being *as* Father, *as* Son and *as* Spirit.

We can now formulate: God *is* concrete in the harmony of his modes of being *as* he who brings to speech, as he who he chooses to be. Shorter: God is concrete in that he himself assigns to himself his being *as* Father, *as* Son and *as* Spirit and so corresponds to himself. In this concreteness of God's being is grounded the fact that God can reveal himself and that in revelation there comes a precise correspondence of the involution and convolution of the three modes of being in the *work* of God to 'the involution and convolution of the three modes of being in the *essence* of God'.[150] For in revelation as self-interpretation God manifests himself as object, who – as subject – has brought himself in the concrete unanimity of his being to correspondence (in that he himself assigned to himself his own being). The over-emphasised terminological difference between 'object' and 'subject' means that when God manifests himself in revelation as *he* who he is, this procedure is self-interpretation and must thus be distinguished from the event in which God himself assigns to himself his being as Father, as Son and as Spirit. But in that God himself assigns to himself his being as Father, as Son and as Spirit, he corresponds to himself concretely.[151]

[150] *CD* I/1, p. 374.
[151] Karl Rahner's critical statement, that 'among theologians since Augustine (contrary to the tradition preceding him) it has been more or less agreed that each of the divine persons (if it were only freely willed by God) could become man and that the incarnation of the second Person in particular throws no light on the special character of *this* Person within the divine nature', may on account of Barth's doctrine of the Trinity be regarded as out-of-date (K. Rahner, 'Remarks on the Dogmatic Treatise "De

The explanations should have made it clear that with the doctrine of the Trinity Barth is concerned to prevent the opposing of a *deus nudus* to the *deus incarnatus*. For the dogma of the Trinity 'will not lead us beyond revelation and faith, but into revelation and faith, to their correct understanding'.[152]

Trinitate" ', in: *Theological Investigations* IV, p. 80). Rahner acknowledges the strange fact, that on the one hand every doctrine of the Trinity must stress the differentiation of the three hypostases in God, while on the other hand the concept of the 'hypostasis' in *Christology* is then employed 'as if it is obvious that a "*functio hypostatica*" with respect to human nature could be exercised just as well by another hypostasis of the Trinity . . .' (*op. cit.* p. 80, fn. 6), sn that the distinction of the modes of being in God is not formulated *concretely*. The decisiveness with which Barth confronted this danger will have become clear. Rahner further objects 'that the revelatory communication of the mystery of the Trinity' is understood, correspondingly, only in 'the mode of a purely verbal communication, which does not change the real relationship between the giver (as Triune) and the hearer' (*op. cit.* p. 82, fn. 10). Rahner thus recognizes clearly the defect in this form – to which he objects – of the doctrine of the Trinity as a definitely hermeneutical defect: 'The Trinity is not merely a reality to be expressed in purely doctrinal terms: it takes place in us, and as such does not first reach us in the form of statements communicated by revelation. On the contrary these statements have been made to us because the reality of which they speak has been accorded to *us*' (*op. cit.* p. 98). Thus according to Rahner an 'ontologically real relationship between man and each of the three divine Persons, a relationship which is not mere appropriation (*op. cit.* p. 82), may not be denied. Barth's understanding of revelation as God's interpretation of himself may have done justice to this demand of Rahner's in an exemplary way. At any rate one will not be able to overcome adequately the problems sketched by Rahner as long as one allows the 'ontologically real relationships' between the three divine modes of being and man to be more than 'mere appropriations'. For one has then understood the act of appropriation just as a mere act of signification which does not belong to revelation. Indeed, one must confront the defect which Rahner objects to – that the divine hypostases in God would be formulated only abstractly in their differentiation – precisely by formulating the hypostases of God as concrete modes of being determined by God himself through appropriation, whereby the act of appropriation would be understood as a decisive 'act of the divine life in the Spirit', as God's 'being-in-act'(in the act-word). More precisely: as the act which co-constitutes the divine life of the Spirit, as the act-word of God which concretely articulates God's being-in-act. Without such an understanding of appropriation Barth's doctrine of the *eternal obedience* of the Son of God in the being of the triune God would also be scarcely thinkable. Whether the appropriating is, in a special way, to 'appropriate' to God the Father, would have to be examined.

[152] *CD* I/1, p. 396. The doctrine of the Trinity thus communicates not

It may be shown how precisely the doctrine of appropriation and thus the understanding of the being of God as concrete event fundamentally determine Barth's whole *Dogmatics*, in particular his doctrine of election and later his doctrine of reconciliation.

---

so much conceptions about revelation as rather an engagement with it. 'Engagement' is thereby not to be understood merely 'subjectively' but signifies the original *earnest* preoccupation, while the conception can simply misplace such a preoccupation, namely, in so far as the concipient remains confined in the horizon of his conceptions. Conceptions as such are anything but a guarantee of objectivity; in fact they are rather the objectified form of subjectivism. (Gollwitzer in his polemic against E. Fuchs' ontological priority of 'engagement' misunderstood Fuchs, cf. *The Existence of God*, p. 110; in his most recent work: *Gottes Offenbarung und unsere Vorstellung von Gott*, Munich, 1964, however, he employs in an exemplary way the distinction which Fuchs makes and thereby leaves the misunderstanding behind.) The necessity of conceptions is thereby not doubted.

2

⬤━━━➤

GOD'S BEING-AS-OBJECT

When in the following pages we speak of God's 'being-as-object' then it will be clear from the foregoing discussion that, for Barth, an objectifying of the being of God is certainly not to be understood in the sense that the knowing human subject could himself make God available as an object which may be, or has been, known. To repulse this misunderstanding was indeed an essential function of Barth's doctrine of the Trinity. The doctrine of the Trinity had to lay down the fact that God as the subject of his being is also the subject of his being known and becoming known. This is why for Barth the doctrine of the Trinity stands at the beginning of his *Dogmatics* and hence also at the beginning of the doctrine of God in the narrower sense.

It would not, however, be possible to speak of a *knowledge* of God if in this knowledge the knowing God does not really *know* and thus is not the subject of the knowledge of God. In so far as the knowing man is the *subject* of the knowledge of God, God must be spoken of as the *object* of this knowledge. In this sense talk about God's 'being-as-object' is indispensable. But how far *is* man the subject and hence God the object of the knowledge of God? How far is the talk of God's 'being-as-object' (alternatively of his 'objectivity', as Barth generally formulates it) *theologically* legitimate and necessary and not just a general postulate of theoretical knowledge? The answer which Barth gives to this problem makes clear that the problem of the knowledge of God and that of God's objectivity 'is itself already a part of the doctrine of God because it can definitely consist only in a representation of the being and activity of God'.[1] In

[1] *CD* II/1, p. 32.

our inquiry after the *being* of God we will thus have to concern ourselves with the problem of God's being-as-object in the knowledge of God.

It cannot be too strongly emphasized that Barth speaks of the objectivity of God in no way 'to commend some kind of realism or objectivism'.[2] It is also, in no way, the classical theory of knowledge[3] with its distinction between the subject and object of theoretical knowledge and with its view of the immanence of the consciousness and the objectivity and transcendental-consciousness of the objects of the consciousness, which forms the ground of Barth's exposition of the objectivity of God. 'There can be no doubt about this point. He who in the Bible encounters (!) man in the objectivity of the divine . . . is not one object in the series of other objects of man's cognizance.'[4] God as the object of the knowledge of God differentiates himself from all other objects of theoretical knowledge precisely in his being-as-object so that this being-as-object can *not* be determined from the objectivity of other objects. And in that God in his being-as-object differentiates himself from all other objects of human knowledge, he (!) also differentiates man as the subject which knows God in his being-subject from all other modes of knowing, in which man as the knowing subject stands over against an object which is to be known. The same would also be true with regard to more recent attempts to correct the classical theory of knowledge ontologically (N. Hartmann) or to think back into its essence and so to overcome it at the starting point (M. Heidegger). Not because these attempts are not to be taken seriously, but because, if they are intended to be taken seriously, they cannot undertake the task of making intelligible the possibility of the knowledge of God as 'an utterly unique occurrence in the range of all knowledge',[5] without from the beginning

---

[2] *CD* II/1, p. 13.
[3] With regard to the problem of the classical theory of knowledge in the realm of theological knowledge cf. Gerhard Stammler, 'Das Verhältnis von wissenschaftlicher und theologischer Erkenntnis. Eine erkenntnis-theoretische Studie zur Wissenschaftslehre', *ZPhF* XVII (1963), p. 75f. and p. 245f.; also by Stammler, 'Vom Erkenntnis-Charakter der theologischen Aussagen', *KuD* 9 (1963), p. 259f.   [4] *CD* II/1, p. 15.   [5] *CD* II/ 1, p. 14.

E

ranging themselves 'out of range'. But even the attempt to forsake 'the range of all knowledge' in favour of the knowledge of God remains theologically irrelevant, because the 'separating out' which is effectuated by the knowledge of God takes place only in that 'God (!) "exempts" himself as well as the ... man ... i.e. makes himself known as separated from all other objects. At the same time he also sanctifies man in his relationship to himself, i.e. puts him into a separated position.'[6] 'Separated' here can obviously not mean that God is differentiated from all other objects as a strange and isolated object and on this account demands from man a special attentiveness which makes man forget his surroundings (like a prince in the wilderness). 'Separated' can also not mean that God in the difference between his being and all other being claims the special awareness of his being. God is 'separated' neither as one object from other objects, nor by way of the non-objectivity of being over against all other being. No, God is separated *in* his being-as-object. 'Certainly we have God as an object; but not in the same way as we have other objects.'[7] The mode of his being-as-object differentiates God as object from all other objects. And the mode of his being-as-object determines the uniqueness of his being-as-subject, in which man becomes the subject of the knowledge of God.

(a) God's being-as-object as God's being revealed

God's being-as-object in his being revealed. God is thus the object of the knowledge of God in so far as he has interpreted himself. And in so far as God himself in his revelation has interpreted himself and thus made himself the object of the knowledge of God he has also made man the subject of the knowledge of God. In that the being of God 'comes into play as an object, it first of all creates the subject of its knowledge'.[8]

[6] *CD* II/1, p. 15; cf. pp. 6–7 where Barth stresses 'that everything that is described as "God" on the basis of a free choice cannot possibly be God; and that everything that is declared on the grounds of this presupposition to be the knowledge of God cannot have any reality or possibility as a knowledge of God'.　　　[7] *CD* II/1, p. 21.　　　[8] *CD* II/1, p. 21.

Thus man *is* the subject of the knowledge of God only because and in that he *becomes* (*fit*) this subject. That means, on the one hand, that God's being-as-object is not the result of human objectification of God, but conversely, the being-as-subject of the man who knows God is the result of God's being-as-object which is actually fulfilled as self-interpretation. And that means, on the other hand, that man is subject of the knowledge of God *only in the event* of the knowledge of God, 'of the knowledge of God in its actual fulfilment'.[9] That means at the same time that God's 'objectivity' is likewise to be thought of only as *event*. God *makes* himself objective. He *is* only objective as he who has *made* himself objective. If the event-character of God's being-as-object is ignored, then God remains unknown. The object of the knowledge of God is 'the actual being of God'[10] which is actual being precisely in its being-as-object. Whoever at this point wanted to separate act from being would destroy everything.

God's being-as-object to which corresponds man's being-as subject in the knowledge of God must, however, be determined more precisely. If God's being-as-object is his being revealed, then God is objective in his *word*. For revelation was indeed determined by Barth as God's self-interpretation. But if God is objective in his *word*, then the statement 'that God is known through his word'[11] is true. God's being-as-object thus consists in the fact that God as God has become *expressible*. And the knowledge of God consists in the fact that the God who as God has become expressible comes to speech, in that 'he is considered and conceived by men'.[12] This act in which the God who as God has become expressible introduces himself to the speech of men, is faith.

'Faith is the total positive relationship of man to the God who gives himself to be known in his word . . . It is the Yes which man pronounces in his "heart" when confronted by this God . . . in the light of the clarity that God is *God* and that he is *his* God . . . In this event of faith the knowledge of God is realized' which,[13] in the certainty of faith is 'mediated knowledge'.[14]

[9] *CD* II/1, p. 5. [10] *CD* II/1, p. 22. [11] *CD* II/1, p. 4.
[12] *CD* II/1, p. 9. [13] *CD* II/1, p. 12. [14] *CD* II/1, p. 9.

The being-as-subject of the man who knows God is therefore faith. But since man, as we have seen, is only the subject of the knowledge of God in so far as he is made (*fit*) this subject, faith is not to be understood as a general human capacity for knowledge (*cum assensione cogitare*) by virtue of which man could then still objectify God. Rather 'faith as the positive relationship of man to God . . . comes from God himself' in so far as 'God encounters man in his . . . word'.[15] God comes before man in his word. Faith comes to man from God through his word. Man comes before God in faith. Correspondingly: God is to be known in God's word. God lets himself be known through his word, in that he grants faith. God becomes known in faith. 'Man knows God in that he stands before God.'[16] That means, however, that God's being-as-subject is preserved also in his being-as-object, also there, where he 'enters into the relationship of object to man the subject'.[17] There is here no *unio mystica* or any kind of identity between the subject and the object of the knowledge of God. God in his being-as-object is not 'objectified' so that one could identify oneself with him.[18] Rather, God *remains* in his being-as-object the *deus coram homine* and man *remains* – in that he becomes the subject of the know-

---

[15] *CD* II/1, p. 12.   [16] *CD* II/1, p. 9 (original in italics).
[17] *CD* II/1, p. 9.

[18] The danger of all theological statements still consists in such an objectification and not in the possibility that God as 'the one pole in this relation between God and man' is 'robbed of his own stability', so that 'God "is" now only in the event of this relation' (Gollwitzer, *The Existence of God*, p. 49). All that can take place only at one pole which as such has become objectified. A God who has been objectified as a pole of the relationship between God and man can certainly be robbed of all stability and *explained* as an objectification of the defects of human subjectivity which has been elevated into the positive and superlative (Feuerbach), or as an objectification of human being taken back into its subjectivity (thus the frequently found caricature of R. Bultmann; cf. for example, G. Noller, *Sein und Existenz*, p. 107: 'God vanishes in the ego'). But that can only be true of an objectified God whose being-as-object is *not* thought of radically as *event*. The more radically God's being-as-object is thought of as event, the clearer is the truth that God *remains* he who *makes* himself to be the object, and thus man to be the subject of the knowledge of God. The more radically God is proclaimed as *deus coram hominibus*, the more plainly can man be defined as *homo coram deo*.

ledge of God – the *homo coram deo*. But God and man remain in this relation only as long as they engage in this relation, hence in so far as God becomes expressible as God, and man likewise brings to speech this God as the God who has become expressible. *Without* this speech-act there would indeed be a *unio mystica* of *silence*. In that God interprets himself in his word there is nevertheless an enduring distinction between God and man. God as God differentiates himself from man as man precisely where he reveals himself to man. Faith as the knowledge of God is the acknowledgment of this distinction between God and man which takes place when God comes to be expressed in human *speech*. In this sense the knowledge of faith means 'the union of man with the God who is differentiated from him'.[19] For 'God differentiates himself from man in this event'.[20]

(b) God's being-as-object as sacramental reality

The differentiation of God from man who knows him is at the same time defined by Barth as the differentiation of God's being-as-object in relation to the objectivity of other objects. 'We have all other objects just as first of all we have ourselves; we have them as determinations of our own previously arranged existence and in the previously ordered manner of our own existence.'[21] On the other hand, over against God's being-as-object the position of man is 'the position of a fundamentally and irrevocably determined *subsequence*'.[22] This 'subsequence' of man over against God's being-as-object is, 'the position of *grace*. The knowledge of God as the knowledge of faith occurs in this position or it does not take place at all.'[23] The gracious 'previously' of God's being-as-object over against man who knows God has its '*prae*' over against all other objects in that God in his freedom *makes* himself object for us, *gives* himself to us that we may know him. This object cannot be comprehended[24]

---

[19] *CD* II/1, p. 15.   [20] *CD* II/1, p. 31.   [21] *CD* II/1, p. 21.
[22] *CD* II/1, p. 21.   [23] *CD* II/1, p. 21.
[24] *CD* II/1, p. 182. 'Our viewing and conceiving are not at all capable of grasping God.' For 'our viewing and conceiving are simply we ourselves. But we ourselves have no capacity for fellowship with God.' Cf. also *CD*

(as N. Hartmann describes the act of knowing) unless God in his freedom should permit himself to be comprehended. God's objectivity is his gracious comprehensibility.

God in his being-as-object, however, is comprehended only *sub contrario*. God's being-as-object is *mediately* objective in his revelation 'in which he meets us under the sign and veil of other objects'. Correspondingly, the man who knows God stands 'always indirectly before God. He stands directly before another object, one of the series of all other objects. The objectivity of this other object represents the objectivity of God . . . This other object is thus the medium by which God gives himself to be known and in which man knows God.'[25] That another object ('a part of the objective reality surrounding man which is different from God'[26]) can be introduced as a medium for God's being-as-object is certainly not grounded in the mediating object itself, but in the fact that God consents to use it as such. As a piece of objective reality which God consents to use it is 'in a *special* sense a work of God', so that 'above and beyond its own existence (which is also God's work, of course) it may and must serve to attest the objectivity of God and therefore to make the knowledge of God possible and necessary'.[27] Such an object, from the range of all other objects, which mediates God's objectivity by virtue of the special event in which God himself chooses the object as a medium of the knowledge of God, is a 'special' work of God. This special event guards 'the objectification of God' which 'always occurs concretely in the use of a medium'[28] from becoming a 'sort of atlas of revelation from which we can read off the being of God without God himself speaking to us through it all in his act as the living Lord, according to his free grace'.[29]

II/1, p. 187 where it reads 'that God does not belong to the objects which we can always subjugate to the process of our viewing, conceiving and expressing and therefore our spiritual oversight and control . . . God is incomprehensible'. The possibility of knowing God is thus grounded *extra nos*. God hires out the human capacity for knowledge and gives to it as hired the possibility of the knowledge of God.   [25] *CD* II/1, pp. 16–17.
[26] *CD* II/1, p. 17.   [27] *CD* II/1, p. 17.
[28] *CD* II/1, p. 29.   [29] *CD* II/1, p. 23.

If, as according to Barth, God's being-as-object for the man who knows God can only be viewed and comprehended in the objectivity of a medium which witnesses to God's being-as-object, a medium out of the created reality which surrounds man, then, with Barth, a distinction must clearly be made between God's being-as-object as such and God's creative objectivity which witnesses to his being-as-object. Barth expresses this difference by the conceptual distinction of 'primary' and 'secondary' objectivity.[30] We will have to turn briefly to that which Barth understands by the 'primary objectivity' of God in order to be able to determine adequately God's 'secondary objectivity' which he has for us in his revelation.

Because God in the objectivity of his revelation, in which he lets himself be known to men, *reveals himself as the Lord,*[31] we must, according to Barth, speak of a 'primary objectivity' of God. We have seen that, for Barth, the category of the lordship of God is an expression of the *capacity* for revelation, of the *possibility* of revelation which is grounded in the being of God. This possibility which is grounded in the being of God is disclosed as the actuality of the being of God by an 'inference', theologically. Thereby the basic statement: 'Where the actuality exists, there is also the corresponding possibility',[32] serves Barth's purpose as an ontological axiom which is itself grounded in revelation. Thus precisely in order to understand the objectivity of God in his revelation, Barth infers from this objectivity a 'primary objectivity' of God in God's intra-trinitarian being – an objectivity differentiated from that in revelation. Barth likewise understands this 'intratrinitarian inference' (as I would like to call it) – which basically determines his whole thinking – itself as knowledge of revelation (and not as metaphysical speculation!) which by inference follows and confirms *a posteriori* the self-demonstration[33] in which the God who reveals himself stands before man.

When Barth by this inference-procedure infers a 'primary

---

[30] *CD* II/1, p. 16 passim.   [31] *CD* II/1, p. 44f.
[32] *CD* II/1, p. 5.   [33] *CD* II/1, p. 45.

objectivity' of God, then this signifies that God *becomes* objective to us not only as the Lord, but that he *can* also become objective to us because he is the Lord. This '*can*' or *ability* is an actuality proper to God's being. God's ability is thus inherent in him not only as something future, in the sense of the potentiality of a 'being in potentiality' (δυνάμει ὄν) which is in tension with a 'being in act' (ἐνεργείᾳ ὄν, Aristotle); no, God's ability is *actually* present[34] in him as his power (*Macht*)[35] 'at a stroke and once and for all'.[36] 'God is who he is . . . There is no other being of God behind or beyond this entirety of his being.'[37] This statement contains the theological assertion that the God who reveals himself *as* Lord *is* actually 'the one, supreme and true Lord'.[38] God's being as Lord[39] necessitates talk about a 'primary' objectivity of God. God's primary objectivity' is his glory, his 'actual lordship' in which he is 'the Lord in himself',[40] in which he stands over against himself and knows himself. That 'he is in himself from eternity to eternity the triune God, God the Father, the Son and the Holy Spirit', that is 'the inner strength of his self-demonstration as the Lord'.[41] Because God as the Lord is objective to himself he sets forth his self-demonstration in the 'secondary objectivity' over against men *with compelling force*.

God's intratrinitarian being-as-object comes to realization in the act in which God knows *himself*. In revelation God gives man a share in this event of the knowledge of God and of his truth.[42] This sharing is first made possible through the event of God's knowledge of himself and thus rests on the fact that 'an occurrence takes place in God himself which is, so to say, copied

---

[34] But in fact 'the primary objectivity of God to himself is actuality in his eternal being as the Father, the Son and the Holy Spirit' (*CD* II/1, p. 49).
[35] 'The fact that we know God is his work and not ours. . . . The possibility on the basis of which this occurrence is realized is his divine power' (*CD* II/1, p. 40).   [36] *CD* II/1, p. 61f.   [37] *CD* II/1, p. 51.   [38] *CD* II/1, p. 51.
[39] Barth later differentiates the Lordship of God 'in the sphere of God as the sphere of his own truth' (*CD* II/1, p. 49) in order to see the obedient 'way of the Son of God into the far country' (*CD* IV/1, p. 157) grounded and made possible in the intratrinitarian obedience of the Son to the Father.
[40] *CD* II/1, p. 47.   [41] *CD* II/1, p. 47.
[42] The event in which God knows himself is the truth of this knowledge.

in the revelation in which man participates . . . In revelation itself we again see God's self-knowledge, God's own and original objectivity in the modes of being of the Father and of the Son through the mode of being of the Holy Spirit.'[43] But now in so far as in revelation this event and thus God's own and original being-as-object is 'copied', the sharing in this event becomes an indirect sharing. The indirectness of the sharing in God's knowledge of himself must not be taken to mean that in his revelation God does not give himself to be known by us completely, but 'only in part, as if we still had to await the revelation of another God in another and higher order, or the revelation of the same God in a different form'.[44] *Nothing more, according to Barth, can be added to the knowledge of faith. It will be confirmed eschatologically.*[45]

The indirectness of the sharing in the truth of God consists rather in the fact that God 'gives himself to be known . . . in an objectivity different from his own, in a creative objectivity'.[46] That God gives himself *sub contraria specie* to be known in his work is, for Barth, a *sacramental* subject matter. 'We may say quite simply that revelation means sacrament, i.e. the self-witness of God, the representation of the truth . . . in the form of creative objectivity.'[47] In so far as God reiterates his 'actual objectivity' in the objectivity – which is strange to him – of his creature, God's being-as-object is sacramental reality. God's being-as-object as sacramental reality signifies a *distinction* for the creature which 'in its objectivity becomes the representative of God's own objectivity'. But at the same time – from the beginning – God's being-as-object as sacramental reality is 'for

---

[43] *CD* II/1, p. 51.   [44] *CD* II/1, p. 51.

[45] The 'boundaries of the knowledge of God' do not make the knowledge of God incomplete. For *terminus a quo* and *terminus ad quem* of the knowledge of God consist in the fact 'that in it we have to do with God himself *through God himself*, that in it we have to do with God himself through God himself in insurpassable and incontestable certainty'. The delimitation of the knowledge of God by God himself gives the knowledge of God its perfection. Within this delimitation the proclamation which brings salvation also takes place. 'But what is sufficient for our salvation cannot, as knowledge of God, be other than perfect' (*CD* II/1, pp. 180–1).

[46] *CD* II/1, p. 52.   [47] *CD* II/1, p. 52.

God himself a *renunciation* of the visibility of his distinction over against the creature'.[48] Because God is the *deus revelatus* who graciously distinguishes his creature, he is in his sacramental being-as-object the *deus absconditus*.[49] God in his sacramental being-as-object is the *deus absconditus* in so far as he allows creation, in whose objectivity he is objective, to speak for himself. For God's sacramental being-as-object consists in the fact that 'he permits some one of his creatures or a happening in the sphere and time of the world created by him to speak for him'.[50] God's being-as-object is thus sacramental reality in that God *in* the reality which encompasses us brings himself to speech *through* this reality. God's being-as-object as sacrament means: God speaks of himself in the world, alternatively God speaks with us in human language. Therefore the 'humanity of Jesus Christ as such is the first sacrament'.[51]

[48] *CD* II/1, pp. 54–5.
[49] Similarly, already in 1929, in the article 'Die Lehre von den Sakramenten' (*Zwischen den Zeiten* 7, 1929, p. 439): 'God is unveiled to us in the sign. But just this sign is also his veiling.'   [50] *CD* II/1, p. 53.
[51] *CD* II/1, p. 54. In *CD* IV/2, p. 55 Barth seriously questions whether the glory of Jesus Christ marked out through God's presence is not the *one and only* sacrament of the Christian Church: 'Was it a wise action on the part of the Church when it ceased to recognize in the incarnation, in the *nativitas Jesu Christi*, in the mystery of Christmas, the one and only sacrament, fulfilled once and for all, by whose actuality it lives as the one form of the one body of its Head, as the earthly-historical form of the existence of Jesus Christ in the time between his ascension and return? Has it really not enough to occupy it in the giving and receiving of this one sacrament, whose reality it has to attest to the world in its proclamation and therefore in baptism and the Lord's Supper, but whose reality it has neither in baptism and the Lord's Supper, nor in its preaching, nor otherwise to represent, to repeat, even to put into practice in its action? However we may understand these "sacraments" (and then, of course, the sacramental character of the Church and its action), what was it that really happened, what was hazarded and achieved, when particular "sacraments", or a particular sacramental action and being, were placed *alongside* that *one* which took place and has its being in Jesus Christ?' Cf. p. 40, where the event of the incarnation is understood as '*the* great Christian mystery and sacrament beside which there is, in the strict and proper sense, no other'. As early as 1929 Barth had designated 'the becoming-flesh of the Word in Jesus Christ' as *the* 'great Christian mystery or sacrament' (*Zwischen den Zeiten* 7, 1929, p. 439). When in *CD* IV/2 he sharpens that formulation in order to keep the concept of sacrament for the incarnation, he takes up an old Reformation

'The existence of the *human nature of Jesus Christ*' is as 'first' sacrament the 'basic reality and substance of the creatureliness which he has commissioned and empowered to speak of him, the basic reality and substance of the sacramental reality of his revelation'.[52] From the existence of the man Jesus there stretches '*a sacramental continuity* both backwards . . . and forwards';[53] but this sacramental continuity has its ground exclusively in the existence of the man Jesus, *with* whom it brings other creatures into a history, creatures who *with* 'the attestation which occurred through the man Jesus'[54] witness to God's objectivity. Because the human nature of Jesus (i.e. 'the existence of the man Jesus') *gratia unionis*, 'through its union with the eternal word of God',[55] has in a definitive way attested God in his objectivity, 'the existence of this creature in his unity with God means the promise that other creatures also may attest God's own objectivity in their objectivity, so that to that extent they may be the temple, instrument and sign of God as he is'.[56] The sacramental priority of the man Jesus consists in the fact that God is objective in the existence of this man *uniquely*. But the uniqueness of God's being-as-object in the humanity of Jesus Christ 'means God's self-humiliation and self-alienation' and therewith 'the concealment of his objectivity by the quite different objectivity of the creature'.[57] The *limitation* in which God is sacramentally objective in the objectivity of the creature comes, however, to the benefit of the creature as the sacramental *determination* of the divine being-as-object. The most extreme estrangement from himself which God experiences in the sacramental objectivity of the man Jesus who died on the Cross, comes to the *benefit* of humanity as the most extreme sacramental determination of God's being-as-object.

The sacramental reality as God's creaturely being-as-object is thus a distinction not only for the creature in whose creatureliness God becomes visible and comprehensible (object), but also

---

tradition. Cf. my article: 'Das Sakrament – was ist das?' (*EvTh* 26, 1966, p. 320f.).

[52] *CD* II/1, p. 53. [53] *CD* II/1, p. 54. [54] *CD* II/1, p. 54.
[55] *CD* II/1, p. 53. [56] *CD* II/1, p. 54. [57] *CD* II/1, p. 55.

a distinction of him who (subject) in this creaturely objectivity *knows God*. In that this knowledge of God takes place, God's self-estrangement comes to the benefit of man through the medium of the sacramental reality. That is the act of the *covenant*. 'Revelation occurs in the form of this sacramental reality, i.e. in such a way that God elevates and selects a definite creaturely subject-object relationship to be the instrument of the covenant between himself the Creator and man as his creature.'[58] We have thus to distinguish between the sacramental reality as the *place* of God's being(-as-object) in creation *and* God's being (revealed) which *occurs* in this place, between the sacramental reality *as creation* and the revelation which first of all constitutes God's sacramental reality *as covenant*, between the sacramental reality *as nature* and the presence of God which makes the reality a sacrament *as grace*.

Because creation and covenant, nature and grace, sacramental medium and revelation as such are *not identical*, there is a '*possibility*' that creation will obstruct and obscure the covenant, that nature will usurp grace, that the sacramental medium will itself claim to be revelation, so that no knowledge of God eventuates. 'The very thing can fail to happen which, because this form is given, ought to happen. The direct opposite can even happen.'[59] That is the danger to which God exposes himself when he makes himself sacramentally objective. For in that God *makes* himself sacramentally objective, he *is* sacramentally objective in the sense 'that by his being revealed to us as He and as Thou, he remains hidden from us as I and therefore in the being and essence of his Godhead'.[60] God's

---

[58] *CD* II/1, p. 55.   [59] *CD* II/1, p. 55.

[60] *CD* II/1, p. 58. The thoughtless objection that statements about God's being and essence are impossible (which in view of the expositions in the *Church Dogmatics* would amount to the reproach that Barth intended to accomplish what he himself had declared to be impossible) fails to understand that according to Barth it is God's 'I' that lets himself be revealed and known as 'He' and 'Thou'. The 'hidden God' is only known as the 'hidden God' in revelation, because the *revealed* God *is* the hidden God. Correspondingly, with the God who reveals himself as 'He' and 'Thou' the 'we' of human existence also becomes thematic. Revelation is indeed no exclusive happening, but a transitional communicative one (cf. *CD* IV/3, p. 8).

hiddenness is his *renunciation* which corresponds to the distinction of the creation. As renunciation God's hiddenness is also *grace*. Indeed, 'it is because the fellowship between God and us is established and continues by God's grace that God is hidden from us'.[61]

It remains, finally, to draw attention to the fact that, according to Barth, God's being-as-object in sacramental reality means that God 'presents time to us'.[62] God presents to us 'his time' which he has 'for us': 'revelation time'. God allows us his revelation time, but just 'through the medium of sacramental reality', i.e. 'at the heart of our time'.[63] Thus God *allows* us our time in order to grant us his time in our time and therewith to grant us time for him. That God's being-as-object in the objectivity of the creature allows us *our* time means at the same moment that God's being-as-object is known 'in *reiteration*',[64] that the whole truth which is to be known, 'is always truth for us temporally. It is truth which always needs to be repeated.'[65] To dispute the necessity of reiterating truth would simply be to misunderstand its temporality and the sacramental communication of God's being-as-object. God is objective in time; i.e. 'in ever new forms of his one revelation he walks with us, ahead of us',[66] so that 'our standing before God in truth is a walking before him'.[67]

(c) God's being-as-object as an anthropological existentiale*

If God's being-as-object in the creaturely objectivity signifies that God presents to us his time in that he permits us our time,

[61] *CD* II/1, p. 183. [62] *CD* II/1, p. 62. [63] *CD* II/1, p. 62.
[64] *CD* II/1, p. 61. [65] *CD* II/1, p. 62.
[66] R. Bultmann can similarly describe faith 'in the transcendent presence of God' when he says 'that faith in the transcendent presence of God can find its expression in speech about the "transformations of God", – an expression which Ernst Barlach has chosen in order to say that the paradox of the presence of God in this world attains shape in a constantly new form . . .' ('Der Gottesgedanke und der moderne Mensch', *ZThK* 60, 1963, p. 344f.). [67] *CD* II/1, p. 62.
* In the philosophy of Martin Heidegger [cf. *Sein und Zeit* (Tübingen, 1927); ET, *Being and Time* (London, 1962)] *existentialia* are the basic structures of human existence. – Tr.

then God's being-as-object has anthropological significance. The anthropological significance of God's being-as-object consists in the fact that God through his being-as-object brings our existence into a definite relationship with his existence. Where God shows himself as object of human knowledge, there he brings human existence into the 'relationship of love and fear to his existence'.[68] That God is objective, therefore, signifies anthropologically, that we may love God above all else and must fear him above all else. In his being-as-object God is there for us, presents to us his time. He so shows himself as he who is worthy of our love; and since he is not different from the form in which he shows himself, he is worthy of love. In his being-as-object God is at the same time with us, allows us our time. He creates therewith 'in us the possibility . . . of loving him'.[69] Since God is not bound to give us this freedom to love, but grants it as love, then it remains true that because we *may* love God above all else, we *must* fear him above all else. 'The man who loves God knows that it is a permission which he has not taken for himself but which is given to him . . . And for that very reason he will fear him as the One without whom he may not love, and as the One whom not to love must mean his own end in terror.'[70]

In that we know God in his being-as-object as the One whom we may love above all else and therefore must fear above all else, 'our existence is actually brought into that relationship' of love and of fear.[71] In his being-as-object God makes it his concern that we do not objectify him as an object but respect in his being-as-object the act which constitutes this being. God makes it his concern 'that we ourselves become a correspondence of

---

[68] *CD* II/1, p. 39.   [69] *CD* II/1, p. 33.

[70] *CD* II/1, p. 33ff. The grounding of the necessity to fear God within the permission to love God is characteristic for Barth's understanding of the relation between law and Gospel. That the love of God and the fear of God owe their existence to God's being-as-object in Jesus Christ points back beyond this to the oneness of Gospel and law in the event of God's revelation. For Barth Gospel and law are *two modes of the one word of God* with which we have to do in the sacramental objectivity of the man Jesus as the Word of God.   [71] *CD* II/1, p. 39.

this act, in ourselves and our whole existence, and therefore that our considering and conceiving become the human act corresponding to the divine act'.[72] This human act is called faith. It takes place in that we love and fear God above all else.

That God in his being-as-object makes this relationship of our existence to God's existence (which as the relationship of faith is the relationship of the love of God to the fear of God) his concern, gives God's being-as-object its anthropological-existential significance. God in his being-as-object is he who makes man his concern, in that he makes the love and fear of God which determine human existence his concern. In fact, therefore, every legitimate statement about God's being-as-object must at the same time be a statement about man. That is true for God's sacramental being-as-object but it has its consequences also for the statements about God's – as Barth terms it – 'primary objectivity', as is made clear by the intratrinitarian foundation of the doctrines of election and reconciliation in the *Church Dogmatics*.

It would be wise to defend our exposition of God's being as an anthropological *existentiale* against two objections. The first objection arises from within the Barthian 'School' in so far as one might fear there that God's being – understood as an anthropological *existentiale* – might be dissolved in human existence, alternatively, perverted into the 'whence of my frantic life'. Against that it must be said that God's being in its ('secondary') objectivity was designated as an anthropological *existentiale* because we learned so to understand this objectivity that here God, in that he makes himself objective, is fully in action as he who determines human existence to the love and fear of God and thus as he who makes the love and fear of God his concern. God's being as such is not an anthropological *existentiale*. Nevertheless, human existence is certainly constituted as such through this *existentiale*. But this means that human existence is constituted *extra nos* and in this constituting is determined in the act of the love and fear *of God* to be a *nos extra nos esse*.

Here, however, the other objection suggests itself, which is to be expected from the Bultmannian school. *Existentialia* count as expressions of ontologically neutral structures. The love and fear of God, however, are specific acts of Christian existence, hence ontically-*existentiell* realizations of human existence. Now, to be sure, we have

[72] *CD* II/1, p. 26.

not called the love and fear of God an anthropological *existentiale*, but rather God's being-as-object as the being of him who makes the fear and love of God his concern. Yet over against this determination the objection returns even more acutely. For God, as he who makes our love and fear of God his concern, can only be grasped in the event of the love and fear of God, so that to speak of the being of God as an anthropological *existentiale* appears senseless. Against this may be said that God *is* he who makes the love and fear of God his concern and he who thus determines constitutively human existence even when human existence does *not* come to realization as the act of the love and fear of God. The love and fear of God is only possible at all because and in so far as human existence is constituted through the being of God as he who makes the love and fear of God his concern. A deficient love and fear of God is a love and fear of God which is constantly denied and thus always sin. But sin is, certainly *in the face of* God's being-as-object as he who makes the love and fear of God his concern, an *impossible* possibility; nevertheless, *through* the determining of human existence unto the love and fear of God alone, sin becomes an impossible *possibility*. Luther's statement: 'To what you give your heart and in what you trust, that is actually your God', is true in its positive and negative meaning precisely because the 'just God' *is* he who makes the love and fear of God in human existence his concern. And in so far as human existence constitutes itself through the setting of the heart upon something (*ponere seipsum extra se*) it is indeed always constituted through God's being-as-object. Nihilism and atheism, judged theologically, are only made possible ontologically (just like faith) through God's being-as-object, even if (unlike faith) just as the possibility excluded from the beginning, negated by God and in so far rendered impossible.[73] Therefore we call God's being-as-object an anthropological *existentiale*. The appellation can, however, be waived so long as along with the concept the essential fact is not abandoned. To this essential fact belongs, certainly, a unity of agreement that God's covenant is the inner ground of his creation.

The distinction between the theology of Karl Barth and that of Rudolf Bultmann is therefore not grounded in the assertion that Barth with his theological statements abstracts from the anthropological relation given in revelation, while Bultmann,

[73] Cf. *CD* IV/1, p. 747 where Barth speaks of the ontological necessity of faith. Cf. also p. 480, where it is maintained that man cannot become godless ontologically.

conversely, dissolves theological statements in anthropological ones. Such descriptions label the theology of both theologians superficially and thus completely misunderstand them. The distinction may rather be seen in the fact that Barth believes a distinction must be made in the intratrinitarian being of God between God's being-as-object in his revelation as 'secondary objectivity' and a 'primary objectivity' which makes possible this 'secondary objectivity', while Bultmann holds that inquiry after the possibility (which is grounded in God) of revelation is forbidden. To understand this point it is necessary to perceive that Barth in his inquiry after the possibility of revelation does not intend to inquire beyond the boundary of revelation, but rather sees himself compelled to this inquiry on the ground of revelation. But he can then in no way abstract from this that all further theological statements are anthropologically relevant. One must nevertheless remember that, for Barth, the anthropological relevance of theological statements is not the criterion of their truth. The criterion of the truth of theological statements is, for Barth, given rather in the fact that in all theological statements the freedom of the subject of the revelation remains safeguarded. Conversely, for Bultmann, the anthropological relevance of theological statements is the criterion of their truth, because for him, revelation is constantly an eschatological happening which as such becomes event in an historical (*historisch*) 'that'.[74] It amounts to the 'paradoxical identity',[75] that an historical (*historisch*) 'that' becomes historically (*geschichtlich*) significant as eschatological event. Bultmann clings to the '*est*' of this paradoxical identity while for Barth according to the distinction of God's 'primary' and 'secondary' objectivity' God himself has actually come into the picture[76] but 'only' in his work which is the sign that points to him. For

[74] Cf. G. Ebeling: *Theologie und Verkündigung. Ein Gespräch mit Rudolf Bultmann* (Tübingen, 1962), p. 115f.; ET, *Theology and Proclamation. A Discussion with Rudolf Bultmann* (London, 1966), p. 118f. – 'The Mere "That" and the Doctrine of Anhypostasis'.
[75] Cf. G. Bornkamm: 'Die Theologie Rudolf Bultmanns in der neueren Diskussion', *Theol. Rundschau*, N.F. 29, 1963, p. 134f.
[76] Cf. *CD* II/1, p. 39; and *Fides quaerens intellectum*, ET, p. 23.

F

Barth Jesus' being-man is also in this sense 'sacramental reality', parable. What finally separates Barth from Bultmann is the same reservation which Barth also brings forward over against Luther's teaching on the Holy Communion: God's presence in the parable of sacramental reality must not be allowed to lead to equating God with our reality[77] if God is not to be objectified by man. The intention which bound Barth and Bultmann in their common beginnings[78] has thus remained unchanged in them both. Basically distinct, on the other hand, are their ways of thinking which led both theologians to differ from each other. The problem of the relation of Karl Barth's theology to that of Rudolf Bultmann's is only set out systematically and adequately when 'analogy' and 'paradoxical identity' are contrasted with each other.[79]

[77] Cf. 'Ansatz und Absicht in Luthers Abendmahlslehre', in: *Zwischen den Zeiten*, 1923, IV, p. 17f.; also 'Die Lehre von den Sakramenten', *Zwischen den Zeiten*, 7, 1929, p. 456.

[78] Cf. G. Bornkamm, *op. cit.* p. 85.

[79] Bultmann also speaks concerning the possibility of analogical speech about God's actions (Bultmann's concluding summary in *Kerygma und Mythos* II, p. 196), but characteristically under the presupposition of faith which maintains the '*paradoxical* identity' of happenings in the world with the divine action. The attempt of Schubert M. Ogden ('Zur Frage der "richtigen" Philosophie', *ZThK* 61, 1964, p. 103) to make the thought of analogy decisive in Bultmann's thinking is hardly convincing. It is no accident that the clarification of the thought of analogy which he hoped Bultmann would provide was *not forthcoming*.

3

GOD'S BEING IS IN BECOMING

(a) God's being-in-act

In discussing the problem of the knowledge of God Barth had already emphasized that in the event 'of the knowledge of God whose *subject* is God the Father and God the Son through the Holy Spirit', 'we men are taken up into this event as secondary, subsequent subjects'.[1] The taking up of man into the event of the knowledge of God is grounded in the taking up of man into the event of the being of God. That sounds strange and is in no way thought of by Barth in the sense of a θεοποίησις [deification] of man's being. The taking up of man into the event of God's being is rather the act of man's salvation. And 'salvation is more than being. Salvation is fulfilment, the supreme, sufficient, final and indestructible fulfilment of being. Salvation is the perfect being which is not proper to created being but is still future. . . . To that extent salvation is its *eschaton* . . . being which has a *share* in the being of *God* . . . not a divinized being, but an *eternal* being which is hidden in God.'[2] The taking up of man into the event of the being of God, the taking up which comes to man as salvation from God confronts us once more with the problem of

---

[1] *CD* II/1, p. 181: 'Therefore we are not speaking only of an event which takes place on high, in the mystery of the divine Trinity. We are indeed speaking of this event, and the force of anything that is said about the knowledge of God consists in the fact that we speak also and first of this event. But we are now speaking of the *revelation* of this event on high and therefore of our *participation* in it. We are speaking of the *human* knowledge of God on the basis of this revelation and therefore of an event which formally and technically cannot be distinguished from what we call knowledge in other connections, from human cognition.'

[2] *CD* IV/1, p. 8.

God's being. For we have to inquire after the *ground* of the taking up of man into the event of God's being. In this inquiry we are confronted with the special event in the self-relatedness of God's being, an event which determines the concreteness of God's being with respect to man, the 'Election of Jesus Christ'. The election of Jesus Christ implies a divine decision concerning God's being whose explicit consequence will be discussed as the 'suffering of God'. But in the election of Jesus Christ as well as in the suffering of God it is a question of 'God's being-in-act'. We shall do well therefore to recollect briefly the definition of this concept of being which Barth undertakes in his doctrine of God under this heading.

After what has been said about revelation as the self-interpretation of God, it will be clear that Barth's exposition of God's being does not employ the concept of being in the sense of a general doctrine of being. Barth's *Dogmatics* makes ontological statements all along the line. But this *Dogmatics* is not an ontology; at any rate not in the sense of a doctrine of being formulated from a general concept of being within which the being of God (as highest being, as being-itself, etc.) would be treated at the appropriate place. Barth raises sharp protest, from which in fact he in no way exempts the old-Protestant orthodoxy, against the 'threatened development of the doctrine of God into a doctrine of being'.[3] Nevertheless Barth does not shrink from making ontological statements. All statements about the knowledge of God and thus about God's being-as-object possess a thoroughly ontological character. That is no less true for Barth's doctrine of the Trinity. Therefore the employment of the concept of being for the *Dogmatics* is unavoidable. Barth will 'not yield to a revulsion against the idea of being as such but will rather take up the concept with complete impartiality'.[4] However, the concept of being which is taken up in all impartiality must immediately be adequately defined, both theologically and ontologically, if it is to be suited for responsible speech about God's being. But that means, for Barth, that the concept of being must be measured by the

[3] *CD* II/1, p. 260.   [4] *CD* II/1, p. 260.

revelation of God. God's revelation is the criterion of all ontological statements in theology. In the face of this criterion ontological statements in theology are not only legitimate but indispensable.[5]

Revelation means God's interpretation of himself as Father, Son and Holy Spirit. We have now become acquainted with Barth's Trinitarian explication of this subject matter and from this knowledge we may already note how Barth in the exposition of God's being theologically defines the concept of being by the criterion of revelation. The being of God was thought of in the oneness of three modes of being differentiated from one another. God's being is thus *self-related* being. As being it is structured as a relationship. But this relational structuring of God's being constitutes God's being not in the sense of an independent impersonal structure[6] in relation to this being; indeed, the modes of God's being which are differentiated from one another are so related to each other that each mode of God's being *becomes* what it *is* only together *with* the two other modes of being. The relational structuring in God's being is the expression of varying 'original-relations' and 'issues' of God's being. God's being as the being of God the Father, Son and Holy Spirit is thus a *being in becoming*. The doctrines of *perichoresis* and appropriation within the three modes of God's

[5] Against Otto Weber, whose main objection against Barth's theology is directed against the ontological character of theological statements in the *Church Dogmatics* (cf. *Grundlagen der Dogmatik*, 2 vols.; Neukirchen, 1955, 1962, passim) whereby at the same time he makes the criticism that Barth dissolves the paradox of the Christian revelation 'in that he introduces the paradox already, as it were, into God's essence' (II, p. 184). In Barth's sense it would indeed have to be pointed out that ontological statements in theology do not imply a theological ontology (a postulate of Heinrich Ott's; cf. the conclusion of his book *Geschichte und Heilsgeschichte in der Theologie Rudolf Bultmanns*, Tübingen, 1955).

Barth's understanding of paradoxical speech only as a *modus loquendi* without particular worth is based on the fact that he attempts to think out God's revelation entirely from its source in God. Thereby the paradox of revelation is not actually introduced into God's essence; on the other hand the statement that *God* is subject and predicate of revelation is taken seriously in a consistent way: God reveals himself.

[6] *Cf. CD* II/1, p. 299: 'In God there is no it that is not he himself.'

being differentiated from each other and united as 'threehood' defined this knowledge: God's being is in becoming. And God is already 'ours in advance' in that his being is a being in becoming from eternity. Already in advance – therefore Barth speaks of the *being* of God: 'God is not subsumed in the relation and attitude of himself to the world and us as actualized in his revelation',[7] but God is fully subsumed in his relation and attitude to himself as Father, Son and Holy Spirit. God is, however, already in this his being no other than he who he is in his revelation. He is thus in this his being already *ours* in advance, and therefore the statement is true: God's being is *in becoming*.

This statement, too, will certainly require to be defined further. To begin with it signifies that God in his being is indeed to be thought of as *subject*, but subject in no other sense than as *active* subject. God *is* active. In this sense Barth also defines the concept of being with respect to God's being, in his doctrine of God, whose fundamental chapter is deliberately headed with the concept 'The *Reality* of God'[8] – 'a concept which holds together being and act and does not tear them apart like the concept of "essence" '.[9] Barth's definition of the concept of being is likewise theologically and ontologically significant. It is theologically decisive that the concept of being is measured by the concept of God in such a way that the concept of God is won anew from the interpretation of revelation as the self-interpretation of God. Revelation is an event. It is a factual event in so far as history belongs to revelation, just as in a proposition a logical predicate belongs to a logical subject. It is, however, not the predicate of history which makes *possible* revelation as event, but revelation as event is *possible* because revelation of itself demands the predicate of history; and in so far as this predicate joins itself to this subject – it belongs to the essence of revelation *that* history as the predicate joins itself to revelation as the

[7] *CD* II/1, p. 260.

[8] *CD* II/1, p. 262.

[9] However, on the same ground M. Heidegger prefers precisely the concept of *essence* (*Wesen*) since this also allows itself to be thought of verbally in the sense of being present (*Anwesen*).

subject – revelation is real, revelation *takes place*.[10] That has consequences if on the basis of the understanding of revelation as event the being of God is also understood as event. 'Seeking and finding God in his revelation, we cannot avoid the action of God and resort to a God who is not active', so that 'with regard to the being of God, the word "event" or "act" is *final*, and cannot be overruled or in any way set in question'.[11] But just as revelation immediately qualifies the predicate of history which belongs to it as a *special* history which *decides* over all other history, so also the being of God which is to be thought of as event is 'not any event, not event in general' but is immediately qualified as 'an event which as such is in no sense to be transcended'.[12] '*Actus purus* is not sufficient as a description of God. To it there must be added at least "*et singularis*".'[13]

The distinctiveness of God's being as event is worked out by Barth in a thought-process which draws an ever-narrowing circle. God's being must not be thought of as event in such a way that God's actuality is differentiated from all other actuality only as 'its essence or principle', because while God 'is differentiated from all other actuality, he is still connected to it'.[14] God's being as event would remain only in a 'dialectical transcendence which, however strictly it may be understood, must always be understood with equal strictness as immanence'.[15]

[10] Revelation as such does *not* belong to history. For revelation is not a predicate of history, but history is a predicate of revelation. Cf. *CD* I/2, p. 58.
[11] *CD* II/1, p. 263.   [12] *CD* II/1, p. 262.
[13] *CD* II/1, p. 264.   [14] *CD* II/1, p. 264.
[15] *CD* II/1, p. 264. The dialectic of the statement 'that *the transcendent* must not be sought and cannot be found above or beyond the world, but *in the midst of this world*' (R. Bultmann, 'Der Gottesgedanke und der moderne Mensch', *ZThK* 60, 1963, p. 342), is not to be understood in the sense of this 'dialectical transcendence' and thus not 'just as the idea is both immanent in the phenomenon and transcendent to it' (*CD* II/1, p. 264), but expresses the 'paradox' 'that the event of revelation is at the same time both a historical as well as an eschatological event' (Bultmann, 'Der Gottesgedanke und der moderne Mensch', p. 342, fn. 26). The relation between history and eschatology must then certainly be strictly defined. Bultmann's book *History and Eschatology* (The Gifford Lectures 1955, Edinburgh, 1957) leaves us in no doubt that the eschatological event decides the history within which it takes place. But if history should decide the eschatological event which

Over against the supposition of such a dialectical transcendence of God, which must necessarily lead to paradoxical statements about God's being, God's being is to be thought of as free from all dialectic, as '*free* event, *free* act, *free* life in itself'.[16]

We must of course at once ask further what is the special feature of this freedom, what is 'therefore the specific freedom of the event'[17] of God's being. Barth determines the special feature of the freedom of the event in what and as what God is, in distinction from events of nature and in distinction from the spiritual freedom of the Spirit as the freedom of an act which is to be comprehended 'only in the oneness of Spirit and nature'.[18] 'We speak of an action, of a deed, when we speak of the being of God as a happening.'[19] The *act*, however, as the specific determination of the free event, as that which God's being is to be understood, is no dumb act but an act-word. 'Indeed the peak of all happening in revelation, according to Holy Scripture, consists in the fact that God speaks as an I, and is heard by the Thou who is spoken to. The whole content of this happening consists in the fact that the *Word* of God became flesh. . .'[20] The understanding of the act in which God *is*, as *act-word*, leads us to understand God's being 'in accordance with the happening of revelation as . . . "*being in person*" '.[21]

God's being in person is in a specific way *free* event in so far as it is not only 'being moved in itself and therefore motivating being', 'but being which is *self-moved*'.[22] That means the *freedom of decision* belongs to the being of God as event. Decision belongs to the being of God not as something which is added to this being, but as event God's being *is* his own decision. 'The fact that God's being is event, the event of God's act, necessarily . . .

takes place within it then this event would become thematic only as a fact of the past. And 'Jesus Christ is the eschatological event not as an established fact of past time, but as repeatedly present, as addressing you and me here and now in preaching' (pp. 151–2).

[16] *CD* II/1, p. 264. It should be remarked that the concepts 'transcendence' and 'immanence' do not in any way form a contradictory opposition to each other, but determine one another logically and reciprocally. Cf. Gerhard Stammler, 'Ontologie in der Theologie?', *KuD* 4 (1958), p. 143f.

[17] *CD* II/1, p. 265.   [18] *CD* II/1, p. 267.   [19] *CD* II/1, p. 267.
[20] *CD* II/1, p. 267.   [21] *CD* II/1, p. 268.   [22] *CD* II/1, p. 268.

means that it is his own conscious, willed and executed decision.'[23] What was already worked out in the doctrine of the Trinity is now corroborated by the working out of a concept of being appropriate to God: God's being is constituted through historicality. For the being of God in its 'decision, and therefore personal being, is the being of God in the modes of being of the Father and the Son and the Holy Spirit' in which God lives 'from and by himself'.[24] And because God lives solely from and by himself, the understanding of God's being as Person is no 'personification' within an undertaking effectuating itself as 'personalism contra ontology' but an understanding of being in the *actual* sense alone appropriate to God. For 'strictly speaking, *God alone* can be said to live' (*propriissime solus Deus vivere dici potest*).[25]

Barth hastens to make the *substantial* determination of the act which constitutes God's being immediately follow this *formal* determination of the concept of being in speaking of God's being-in-act. For the tautology 'God is God' is only to be resolved through a substantial determination of this act. The revelation of God, as the substantial determination of the act in which God is, is the resolution of this tautology. Revelation, however, resolves the tautology 'God is God' in such a way that God's own decision is to be understood not only as a decision for *God*, but precisely as a decision for God, which is also a decision for *man*. God 'certainly wills to be God and he does not will that we should be God. But he does not will to be God for himself nor as God to be alone with himself. He wills as God to be for us and with us, who are not God. Inasmuch as he is himself and affirms himself, in distinction and opposition to everything that he is not, he places himself in this relation to us. He does not will to be *himself* in any other way than he is in this *relationship*.'[26] God's setting-himself-in-relation (being as event) to us qualifies God's act of revelation *as love*. God acts as *the loving one* in that he will be ours. But since God in his being as

---

[23] *CD* II/1, p. 271.   [24] *CD* II/1, pp. 271–2.
[25] *CD* II/1, p. 272. Can and must one not then also say: 'Strictly speaking, *God alone* can be said to have died' (*propriissime* SOLUS DEUS *mortuus esse* dici potest)?   [26] *CD* II/1, p. 274.

Father, Son and Holy Spirit is also already ours in advance, then in analogy to God's relationship *ad extra*, it must also follow from the relationship of God's three modes of being to one another, that God *acts as the loving One*. 'In itself, first and last, it will always be this and no other relationship. God wills and does nothing ambiguously, but only one thing – *this* one thing.'[27] And this one thing is 'God's highest good, that which distinguishes his act as divine, and therefore also his person as divine',[28] namely God's loving in which he, in his way, is *the* One,[29] the One who loves in freedom. Barth himself points out expressly that this knowledge is founded on the doctrine of the Trinity by the proposition of the *perichoresis*[30] of the three divine modes of being, which is the ontological basis for the *analogia relationis* between God's being for himself and his being for us.

It would be stimulating to follow Barth's expositions on 'God's being as the loving one' and 'God's being in freedom' in detail. But for the goal that we pursue, what has been said so far will suffice. Yet it will still be profitable to test our proposition 'God's being is in becoming' on Barth's exposition of God's primal decision effectuated in the election of Jesus Christ, and on Barth's disputed thesis of God's passion. We have to do here and there with the extremest but indispensable consequences of that understanding of God's being which we have thus far expounded.

(b) God's primal decision

God's being in act was so understood, that God is his decision. Decision sets relationship; for it is as such a setting-oneself-in-relationship. It is a necessary peculiarity of Barth's *Dogmatics* that God's setting-himself-in-relationship in this way, looks inward and outward at the same time. That is based on Barth's understanding of revelation as the self-interpretation of God in which God is his own 'double'. And so it is not surprising when this double structure of the single being of God finds its rightful place in the doctrine of election expounded in the *Church*

[27] *CD* II/1, p. 275.   [28] *CD* II/1, p. 275.
[29] *CD* II/1, p. 284.   [30] *CD* II/1, p. 297.

Dogmatics. We understood the single being of God in its double structure as a being in correspondence. And we saw in the proposition 'God corresponds to himself' God's being as the One who loves grounded in freedom. The proposition paraphrases just therewith that historicality of God's being which reiterates itself in the historicality of revelation. This point is expressed by Barth's exposition of God's primal decision, which is coupled – not by chance – with the concept of primal history. God's primal decision is understood by Barth as God's *election in grace*.

As the 'sum of the Gospel' and the 'very essence of all good news'[31] God's election in grace is the beginning of 'all the ways and works of God'.[32] In his ways and works God sets himself in relationship. In speaking of a beginning of these ways and works we mean a relationship of God to that which he is not. For God himself 'has indeed no beginning'.[33] It is thus a question of the beginning of God's *opera ad extra*. But the election in grace as the beginning of all the ways and works of God is not only an *opus Dei ad extra*, more precisely, an *opus Dei ad extra* EXTERNUM,[34] but at the same time an *opus Dei ad extra internum*. For election as election is not only an election effected by God and in so far an election which also certainly affects him, but it is at the same time a decision which affects God himself 'because originally God's election of man is a predestination not merely of man but of himself'.[35] If then the decision of the election in grace not only affects the elected man but at the same time also affects God originally, then dogmatically the next step is to treat the doctrine of predestination as a part of the *doctrine of God*.

The supralapsarian feature – to which Barth after much consideration attributes a relative pre-eminence over all infralapsarianism – which suggests itself in the doctrine of election is,

---

[31] *CD* II/2, pp. 13–14.   [32] *CD* II/2, p. 3.   [33] *CD* II/2, p. 102.

[34] Barth praises it as a happy inconsistency of the old Protestant orthodoxy that in spite of its presupposition of a concept of God defined as *ens simplex et infinitum*, according to which 'God may be everything in the way of aseity, simplicity, immutability, infinity etc., but not the living God', it could also speak of *opera Dei ad extra* INTERNA, of an INTERNA *voluntatis divinae actio* (cf. *CD* II/2, p. 79).   [35] *CD* II/2, p. 3.

however, in its metaphysical tendency immediately caught up by the concrete historical determining of the elected man Jesus. It will be shown that Barth's Christological basis for the doctrine of election makes a radical correction of the presuppositions of the traditional supralapsarianism. Thus he escapes the danger which is inherent in supralapsarian thinking of turning both the electing God (with the doctrine of the *decretum* ABSOLUTUM[36]) and the history of man (predestined either to election or rejection) into something metaphysical. And it will be shown that the supralapsarianism whose 'historical form has to be drastically corrected and supplemented',[37] and which was brought by Barth to its rightful place, permits the being of God and the historical being of man to be thought of in the doctrine of God together in such a way that the demand 'to think of God's eternity as historicality without surrendering the thought of God as Creator'[38] is fulfilled in an extremely precise sense. For in God's election in grace, which is understood as decision for the man Jesus, this man (as representative of men) and God are with one another in eternity. We have therefore to understand this decision as God's 'primal decision' which determines irrevocably God's being-in-act, or rather, in which *God* determines irrevocably his being-in-act. This self-determining of God is an act of his self-relatedness as Father, Son and Holy Spirit. It is, however, *at the same time* an attitude and relation of God to man and, indeed, 'the attitude and relation in which by virtue of the decision of his free love God wills to be and is God. And this relation cannot be separated from the Christian conception of God as such. The two must go together if this conception is to be truly Christian.'[39]

It is thus necessary to inquire more precisely into that primal decision which originally[40] determines the being of God and of

---

[36] Reproached by Barth as an 'idolatrous concept' (*CD* II/2, p. 143).

[37] *CD* II/2, p. 143.

[38] Cf. R. Bultmann (following the article by Schubert M. Ogden), *ZThK* 60 (1963), p. 346.   [39] *CD* II/2, p. 9.

[40] The fact that through God's election in grace man also has been made the subject of a decision in an original way, imparts to the covenant its pre-eminence over the creation which as the 'external basis of the covenant'

man. So much can be said already:

1. God relates himself to himself in that he determines himself to be the electing one;
2. God relates himself to man in that he determines him to be the elected one.

Both statements are, however, in their generality no appropriate expression of God's primal decision. For with these statements the doctrine of election would be based abstractly with respect to the electing God and abstractly with respect to the elected man. '*Latet periculum in generalibus*!'[41] Thus both the electing God as well as the elected man must be determined *concretely*. But the electing God and the elected man can only be determined concretely when the *attitude and relation* of God implicit in God's primal decision is determined concretely. The *attitude and relation* implicit in God's primal decision lets itself be based only on the ground of revelation, which for Barth means Christologically. Accordingly, Barth comprehends in the name Jesus Christ the electing God, the elected man and God's attitude and relation which determines God to be the electing One and man to be the elected one. 'Jesus Christ is the decision of God in favour of this attitude or relation. He is himself this divine relation.'[42] In this relation, which is Jesus Christ, God and man are by each other. For in this relation, which is Jesus Christ, God relates himself to the man Jesus. And 'this man and the people represented in him are creatures and not God'.[43] But at the same time this Jesus Christ is 'a relation of God which is assumed irrevocably . . . a relation in which God is self-determined, so that this determination belongs to him even as everything that he is in and for himself. Without the Son sitting at the right hand of the Father, God would not be God.'[44]

---

is dependent upon this covenant as the 'internal basis of the creation' (cf. *CD* III/1, §41). Consequently it is for Barth forbidden to formulate the election with Thomas Aquinas and the orthodox Reformed tradition which followed him in this as *quaedam pars providentiae* (cf. *CD* II/2, p. 45 and elsewhere).   [41] 'Danger lurks in generalities.' *CD* II/2, p. 48.
    [42] *CD* II/2, p. 7.   [43] *CD* II/2, p. 7.   [44] *CD* II/2, p. 7.

God has, accordingly, in the second mode of being of the Trinity determined himself to be the electing God. 'Jesus Christ is the electing God.'[45] In so far that here one of the three modes of being is *determined* to be the electing God, we shall have to understand God's primal decision as an *event* in God's being which *differentiates* the modes of God's being. In so far as the electing God in the mode of being of the Son, and the elected man Jesus of Nazareth are *one person* in Jesus Christ, the electing God is already determined 'so that as elected *man* he is *himself* the *God* who elects all men in his *own* humanity'.[46] But the event which determines the second mode of being in the Trinitarian being of God to be the electing God may not be thought of without seeing that this event determines the electing *Son of God* to be as elected *man* the God who in his own humanity elects all men.

God's free self-determining in Jesus Christ is thus 'the will of God in action' in so far as

1. God as the electing One has *determined himself* to be this electing God in Jesus Christ.
2. God as the electing One has determined himself to be the electing God *and* elected man in Jesus Christ.
3. God as the electing One in Jesus Christ *elects* the man Jesus.

1. The understanding of Jesus Christ as the electing God introduces the question what makes Jesus Christ the electing God. Barth answers this question with the help of the double-structure – which we have elaborated – of God's being in

---

[45] *CD* II/2, p. 103 (in Barth this statement is in italics); thus from the beginning Barth had taken account of Rahner's concern that already the Trinitarian-theological 'concept of precisely the second hypostasis in God as such' (*Theological Investigations* IV, p. 99) has to make understandable the incarnation of precisely *this hypostasis*. Certainly, in such a way that the 'second hypostasis in God as such' is thought on the basis of revelation and hence, immediately and *concretely*, as a mode of being – which is related so graciously to the elected man Jesus – of the electing God. In this relationship of the second hypostatis, there is repeated the intradivine peace in which the Son in eternity (i.e. the second hypostasis in God 'as such') is obedient to the Father.   [46] *CD* II/2, p. 117.

correspondence. The fact that God in the second mode of being (the Son's) *determines himself* to be the God who elects the man Jesus and chooses oneness with him, makes the Son the object of an election taking place in God himself. But after what has been said concerning the *perichoresis* of God's three modes of being, the Son as elected by the Father to this determination cannot be *object only*. That would immediately conjure up the conclusion of inferiority or even of tritheism. The eternal Son can and may be therefore 'no less the original subject of this electing than he is its original object'.[47] According to Barth the eternal Son participates as subject in the election of the Father in that by his own free divine decision he *accedes* to his *determination* willed by the Father to be the God who elects the man Jesus and chooses oneness with him. The eternal Son *elects* his election by the Father. Thus in the intratrinitarian being he elects *obedience*. 'The obedience which he renders as the Son of God is, as genuine obedience, his own divine, free decision . . . Indeed his own art of electing corresponds most exactly to his being elected.'[48] This *correspondence* in which the Son *accedes* to the will of the Father in the freedom of the Spirit is the 'peace of the triune God'.[49]

The last train of thought confirms the correctness of our interpretation of the Barthian doctrine of the Trinity. We saw how the doctrines of *perichoresis* and appropriation taught us to understand God's Trinitarian being in its historicality. We said that the unity of God's three modes of being proves itself as *concrete* unity when it preserves the *differentiation* of the three modes of being as *concrete* differentiation. This *concrete* differentiation is preserved in that Barth differentiates the Son from the Father in the mode of being of *obedience*. We said further that in that this takes place, the concrete unity articulates itself in oneness with the concrete differentiation of God's modes of being to form the *unanimity as concreteness* of God's being. Barth's exposition of the 'peace of the triune God' in which the Son is 'not less the original subject of that election than he is its original object' is the concrete expression of this subject matter which

[47] *CD* II/2, p. 105.   [48] *CD* II/2, p. 105.   [49] *CD* II/2, p. 105.

we have worked our way through with respect to its formal structure.[50] Our guiding principle of interpretation for Barth's understanding of God's being: 'God corresponds to himself', thus proves itself. In that he corresponds to himself, God *is*. His corresponding *takes place* as God's 'Yes' to himself.[51] This Yes constitutes God's being as co-responding.

2. God does not abandon the correspondence in which God is who he is, when he turns himself to man. Rather God maintains this correspondence to the end in that in this peace of the triune God he determines himself to be in Jesus Christ the electing God *and* elected man. For 'only in this peace of God' can the Son of God who has been determined to be the electing God 'completely fulfil . . . the will of the Father, and thus as man electing, confirm and so to speak repeat the election of God'.[52]

In Jesus Christ the *concreteness* of the divine being is maintained to the end also for man. Therefore Barth strongly resists a basis for the doctrine of election which proceeds from God in *general* (as the subject of the election) and from man in *general* (as the object of the election). Only in the concrete determining of the electing God and only in the concrete determining of the elected man can the *doctrine* of election enable us on our side mentally to maintain the concreteness of God's being which is maintained to the end by God for man. Therefore Jesus Christ as subject and object is, for Barth, also the basis of election.

That leads Barth to the supposition of an *eternal* covenant 'which as it concerns man God made within himself in his pre-temporal eternity'.[53] God the Father determined his eternal Son to be the electing God and as such to be in oneness with man chosen by the Son. This determining is an eternal act. And so Barth can speak of 'the Son of God in his oneness with the

[50] The peace of the triune God is thus *not* the peace of a God who in himself is at rest, but the peace of God's self-moved being. 'Rest' is this peace *as* movement, thus incomparable with the rest of an unmoved mover! 'That God rests in himself does not exclude, but includes the fact that his being is *decision*' (*CD* II/2, p. 175).

[51] Namely in the freedom in which 'from all eternity and in all eternity God affirms and confirms himself' (*CD* II/2, p. 155).

[52] *CD* II/2, p. 105.   [53] *CD* II/2, p. 104.

Son of Man as foreordained from all eternity'.[54] This oneness of
the Son of God and man in Jesus Christ which has been foreordained from all eternity is the 'covenant which God has made
with himself and which for that reason is eternal',[55] and as such
makes possible the incarnation of the Son of God. In this sense
God's primal decision is, at the same time, the 'primal relationship'[56] between God and man in which God turns himself
to man and thus is *already* with man before man was created.
The primal decision constitutes the primal relationship of God
to man and in this primal relationship 'primal history'[57] is

[54] *CD* II/2, p. 104.   [55] *CD* II/2, p. 107.   [56] *CD* II/2, p. 52.
[57] Cf. *CD* II/2, p. 7f. Barth already employs the concept of primal history
in the *Römerbrief* (revised 2nd edition, Munich, 1923), where he speaks of the
'unhistorical', i.e. primal-historical, conditionedness of all history. In the
Prolegomena zur christlichen Dogmatik (Munich, 1927) Barth uses the concept
'to designate the special relation between revelation and history' (p. 230).
He designates as primal history (as 'primal-historical event') 'the Word
becoming flesh, the revelation of God in Jesus Christ' (p. 230) which is
therewith the '*original pattern* or the meaning of all history' (p. 238). Primal
history, which is understood as the Word becoming flesh or as revelation, is
on the one hand more than the 'eternal happening in God himself' (i.e.
'supra-history'), because it is not only an eternal happening in God (supra-
history), but above all a temporal happening (i.e. history) (p. 231f.). On
the other hand it is more than a temporal happening (history), because it is
not only a temporal happening (history), but also an eternal happening in
God (supra-history) (pp. 232-4). This means that primal history (revelation) understood as God's '*opus ad extra*' (p. 231) cannot be related to the
intratrinitarian happening 'as though we should still always find ourselves
in that sphere where God is God in himself, as though it were still always a
question of that eternal happening between Father Son and Holy Spirit'
(p. 231). Rather, conversely, the intratrinitarian happening may be related
to primal history (revelation) 'in so far as that eternal happening in God
takes place also within it' (p. 231).
    In the first volume of his *Church Dogmatics* (I/2) Barth rejects the concept
of 'primal history' because the use of it can give rise to the misunderstanding
that it can mediate the nature of revelation (cf. *CD* I/2, p. 57f.). For
'*revelation is not a predicate of history, but history is a predicate of revelation*' (I/2,
p. 58; likewise in *Die christliche Dogmatik* I, p. 232).
    In the face of this rejection it is surprising that in his doctrine of election
Barth once again takes up the concept of 'primal history'. Does he now
reject his own rejection? Or does the concept take on a new meaning?
Where is its theological place?
    Primal history is now that history which is played out between God and
the one man Jesus (cf. *CD* II/2, p. 8), in that the Son of God takes pon
G

effectuated, in which God, *before* man has been created, *already* relates himself to man. God's being takes place as *historia praeveniens*. In this *historia praeveniens* God determines himself to be ours as one of us. In this determining God's 'being-already-ours-in-advance', which is grounded in the Trinitarian 'being-for-itself', directs itself, so to speak, 'outwardly'[58] in order that in revelation it may come to 'an overflowing of his inward activity and being, of the inward vitality which he has in himself'.[59] The *historia praeveniens* in which and as which this self-determining of God eventuates is Jesus Christ. But then Jesus Christ *is* already in the beginning with God.[60] And precisely this being of Jesus in the beginning with God distinguishes the divine primal history as 'concrete history' which as 'an act of divine life in the Spirit . . . is the law which precedes all creaturely life'.[61]

---

himself the humanity of the man Jesus (cf. *CD* II/2, p. 124). Primal history has reference to the incarnation but precedes this event (cf. *CD* II/2, p. 105). It is 'the attitude and relation in which by virtue of the decision of his free love God wills to be and is God' (*CD* II/2, p. 9), and therefore (in contrast to the *Prolegomena zur christlichen Dogmatik*) has its place in the Trinitarian being of God.

[58] The category 'outwardly' (*ad extra*) employed by Barth following the old theology is a hermeneutical aid directed to man which on its own part requires interpretation. The being of God cannot be distinguished into an inner and an outer side. But the relationship [*Gegenüber*] of the modes of God's being in which God corresponds *to himself* must certainly be distinguished from the opposition [*Gegeneinander-Über*] of God and man in which God makes *his creature* to correspond to himself (God), because God also corresponds to himself in the connection of that relationship with this opposition of God and man.   [59] *CD* II/2, p. 175.

[60] Cf. *CD* II/2, p. 104; cf. also *CD* IV/1, p. 50 and p. 60; *CD* IV/2, p. 31f.

[61] *CD* II/2, p. 184. Gerhard Gloege in his essay 'Zur Prädestinationslehre Karl Barths. Fragmentarische Erwägungen über den Ansatz ihrer Neufassung' (*KuD* II, Berlin, 1957) has marked out (*op. cit.* p. 254) the Christological 'prae' as the formal principle of the Barthian doctrine of election. Gloege's objections are directed precisely against this 'prae' which allows a 'remnant of stability in the thought of God and of revelation' to remain (*op. cit.* p. 239) and leads to a 'making of the Person of Jesus Christ into a principle' (*op. cit.* p. 214, in italics). – That Barth has no intention of thinking of God's being in act without 'stability' has been expressed by Barth himself in his criticism of Peter Barth's thesis of the actuality of predestination (without Barth's Christological grounding!) (Cf. *CD* II/2, p. 188f.). Barth wanted 'to guard against taking the part of the dynamic case against

But if the preceding of the *historia praeveniens* is not to be a matter of indifference and irrelevance for the creaturely life it must as such already be related to the creaturely life. This relatedness without which the HISTORIA *praeveniens* would not be GRATIA *praeveniens* is, for Barth, given in the fact that God, in the being of Jesus Christ who is in the beginning with God, i.e. in that primal history, determines himself to be God *as man*. In this sense God's self-determining is God's 'self-giving' fulfilled 'in his eternal purpose'.[62] The 'eternal divine *fore-ordination*'[63] consists precisely in the fact that God in his self-determining gave his own Son. 'God determined to give and to send forth his Son. God determined to speak his word. The beginning in which the Son became obedient to the Father is with himself.'[64] 'That God has elected fellowship with man for himself' (sc. God) in order 'to elect for man fellowship with himself'[65] (sc. God) is effectuated in the obedience of the Son. In this original double sense Jesus Christ in the *historia praeveniens* of God's election is 'already here . . . in his origin and from all eternity . . . *double predestination*'.[66]

This understanding of double predestination is the ground for the belonging-togetherness of Christology and soteriology, of the doctrine of justification and the doctrine of sanctification in Barth's doctrine of reconciliation. It is important for our context that Barth immediately formulates *concretely* the double predestination also, as 'an act of divine life in the Spirit'. That Jesus Christ *is* this double predestination signifies that God's self-giving is 'a gift made to man' on the basis of God's self-renunciation, in which 'God himself hazards his Godhead and power and domain as God'.[67] The *praedestinatio gemina* is a

---

the static' (*CD* II/2, p. 187). Cf. also Barth's demarcation against the one-sided 'dynamic' Reformed Federal-theology in *CD* IV/1, p. 56. The static-dynamic alternative is rendered obsolete by Barth as is also that of ontology and personalism. The critical phrase about the 'making of the Person into a principle', however, may through Barth's understanding of election as 'the act of divine life in the Spirit' be taken *ad absurdum*.

[62] *CD* II/2, p. 161.   [63] *CD* II/2, p. 161.
[64] *CD* II/2, p. 162.   [65] *CD* II/2, p. 162.
[66] *CD* II/2, p. 162.   [67] *CD* II/2, p. 162.

G 2

praedestinatio dialectica.[68] In Jesus Christ God destined life for man, but death for himself.[69] The dialectic, however, is not sealed up paradoxically but broken open teleologically: 'God wills to lose in order that (!) man may gain.'[70] Barth's doctrine of election is already traced out with reference to the doctrine of justification.[71]

For the *being* of God, this means the 'threat of negation'.[72] For in Jesus Christ the *No* expressed in the justification of the sinner together with the *Yes* to man strikes *from the first*, and therefore once for all, God himself. If from this there results for man the consoling statement that 'the rejection cannot again become the portion or affair of man',[73] then there results for God at the same time the dangerous statement: 'In God's eternal purpose it is God himself who is rejected in his Son.'[74] But since the Son of God is already in the covenant with the *lost* Son of man in the *historia praeveniens*,[75] God already in his eternal being takes the 'threat of negation' seriously. In precisely this way God maintains to the end his Yes to himself as his Yes to man. And precisely in this *maintenance* God's being *remains* in *becoming*.

The becoming in which God's being remains is no medium (μέσον) between non-being and being which participates in

---

[68] Cf. H. Vogel, 'Praedestinatio gemina. Die Lehre von der ewigen Gnadenwahl', in: *Theologische Aufsätze. Karl Barth zum 50. Geburtstag* (Munich, 1936) p. 222f.

[69] *CD* II/2, p. 167.   [70] *CD* II/2, p. 162.

[71] Barth nevertheless understands justification precisely from the viewpoint of election, as God's self-justification. For God's choice 'from all eternity to take to himself and to bear man's rejection is also *God's* prior *justification* in respect of the risk' to which he resolved to expose man by confronting him with annihilation and sin (*CD* II/2, p. 165). Barth's understanding of justification as God's self-justification touches the interpretation recently advocated by Ernst Käsemann in antithesis to Rudolf Bultmann, that Paul's concept of the righteousness of God, which is to be understood as deriving from the apocalyptic tradition, denotes primarily God's power and thereafter God's gift ('Gottes Gerechtigkeit bei Paulus', *ZThK* 58, 1961, p. 367f.).   [72] *CD* II/2, p. 163.

[73] *CD* II/2, p. 167.   [74] *CD* II/2, p. 167.

[75] Cf. *CD* II/2, p. 164; Barth employs the concept 'Son of Man' not in the sense of the apocalyptic tradition of the Old and New Testaments but in the sense of the Patristic Christology.

both. Rather, God's being in becoming excludes non-being as that which is not willed by God. And only as that which is excluded by God does non-being have its own 'independence and value' at all, namely that of the 'being and essence' excluded from God's economy and thus rejected; only so does it possess 'the autonomy and status of *non-being*'.[76] But in that God's being has its ontological place in becoming, God's being *can* encounter the non-being, expose itself to it and in such exposure win through as *suffering* being. The prevenience of the divine being in the primal history of the eternal covenant has as prevenience already as its goal the direct confrontation with *lost* man, and in this confrontation an encounter with death. There the '*Triumph* of the Grace'[77] of God is effectuated. God's encounter with death takes place in Jesus Christ. In Jesus Christ, hell, death and the devil are vanquished. But in so far as Jesus Christ is already with God in the beginning, God also *precedes* non-being, already from eternity,[78] and from the

---

[76] *CD* II/2, p. 170.

[77] G. C. Berkouwer's fine book *The Triumph of Grace in the Theology of Karl Barth* (London, 1956), makes a protest against this attempt which *de facto* desires to comprehend even the incarnation (p. 307). Whoever disputes the confrontation of God's *prevenient* being with non-being must then also dispute Barth's thesis that the Christian has to carry through the confrontation with non-being (as nothingness) by demythologizing it in 'an act of the unbelief which is grounded in faith' (*CD* III/3, p. 521; cf. Berkouwer, *op. cit.* p. 376f.). The less one wants to bring God into relation with suffering, the more intensively will one emphasize the suffering of man. On the other hand, the more radically it is thought 'theopaschitically' that God 'himself tastes damnation, death and hell' (*CD* II/2, p. 164) the more radically can the eschatological existence of the justified man also be understood. 'In Jesus Christ we can see and know this whole sphere of evil as something which has already been overcome, something which yields and retreats, something which has been destroyed by the positive will of God's overflowing glory. And what it is in Jesus Christ it is also in the beginning with God' (*CD* II/2, p. 172; cf. the discussion with Berkouwer, *CD* IV/3, p. 173f.).

[78] These statements about God's prevenience could awaken the impression that God was under an obligation to reveal himself. But just the opposite is the case. The very *obligingness* of God is grace, is an act of his freedom. In his prevenience he is present 'earlier' than everything else which could place him under any obligation. He is, nevertheless, present *for* man and *against* the nothing. He will thus reveal himself, not because of an obligation, but because of *his own self*-obligation in which he is *the One who loves in freedom*.

first it is true: Jesus is conqueror!

3. In that God chooses death for himself he chooses life for man. But life is existence in fellowship with God. In Jesus Christ God has elected man to such fellowship. And since Jesus Christ is the event of the double choice of God, the man Jesus, too, is already with God in the beginning in the primal history of the eternal covenant.

This statement in Barth's doctrine of election sets great difficulties before the reader. For how shall the 'being of Jesus in the beginning with God'[79] be understood? The consequence of this sentence, from the starting-point of the Barthian doctrine of election, is nevertheless clear. If that primal history is real *history* between God and man, then the Son of God cannot be thought of in this history without the man Jesus, and the eternal Word (λόγος) cannot be thought of as the Word without flesh (λόγος ἄσαρκος). If God in this history is *already* with man, then this man on his part must *already* be with God. God's prevenient being is being *imparting* itself as grace. In the sense of such prevenient imparting, the man Jesus *has* already a part in God's eternal being.

Barth's interpretation of John 1. 1f can be a help in understanding the being of the man Jesus with God in the beginning. Barth understands the Word (λόγος) who was with God in the beginning as a *'locum tenens'* for Jesus.[80] The Word (λόγος) has the function of safeguarding the place with God which is to come to Jesus. 'The Word (ὁ λόγος) is unmistakably substituted for Jesus. *His* is the place which the predicates attributed to the logos are meant at once to mark off, to clear and reserve.'[81] 'The force of the threefold "was" (ἦν) in Jn 1, 1 is more than axiomatic. It points to an eternal happening *and* to a temporal: to an external in the form of time, and to a temporal with the content of eternity.'[82] The *event* of the Word (λόγος), however, is

---

Barth wants to speak just as little of a *potentia Dei absoluta* on the one hand, as of a *potentia Dei ordinata* understood as compulsion to revelation on the other hand (cf. e.g. *CD* IV/3, p. 227 and corresponding statements in all volumes of the Church Dogmatics).   [79] *CD* II/2, p. 107.

[80] *CD* II/2, p. 96.   [81] *CD* II/2, p. 96.   [82] *CD* II/2, p. 97.

nothing other than the *expression* 'of the Word which was in the beginning with God and belongs to him'.[83] And this Word is called Jesus. 'It is of this name that we speak.'[84] 'There is nothing thereby projected into eternity',[85] but eternity is planned around this Jesus. And in virtue of this plan in the eternal purpose of God the man Jesus *is* in the beginning with God.

This pre-existent being of the man Jesus must not be interpreted as a 'gnoseological' or 'ideal' being. This being also 'does not belong only passively to the *aeterna Dei praedestinatio*'[86] as Thomas Aquinas taught.[87] The being of the man Jesus in the beginning with God consists rather in the expression of the eternal Word (λόγος): Jesus. And here also it is true that 'he spoke and it came to be' (Ps. 33. 9). In that the electing God has spoken his electing Yes to this man, this man *is* this Yes. He is this Yes not for himself. For himself he is nothing at all. But he *is* this Yes with God.

If I have correctly understood this decisive locus of the Barthian doctrine of election then the being of the man Jesus with God is to be understood in the sense of the doctrine of the *enhypostasis** and *anhypostasis*† of the human nature of Jesus Christ. Barth himself does not explicitly employ this doctrine in connection with the doctrine of election. But if the being of the man Jesus in the beginning with God is not to be understood in the sense of a projection of a temporal existence into eternity, then we must speak of this temporal existence of Jesus in the sense of the *anhypostasis*. Jesus' existence would not be what it is if it were not *already* in the 'eternal decision of God which is the basis and governor of time'.[88] But it is precisely in the eternal decision of God in the sense of the *enhypostasis* that this existence

---

[83] *CD* II/2, p. 98. [84] *CD* II/2, p. 98. [85] *CD* II/2, p. 98.
[86] *CD* II/2, p. 107. [87] *S.Th.* III, qu. 24, art. 1f.

* The doctrine first put forward in the fifth century that the human personality of Christ was included within the *hypostasis* of the incarnate Son of God and that thereby Christ included within himself all the attributes of perfect humanity. – Tr.

† The doctrine that Christ's human nature had no independent centre of personal subsistence of its own. – Tr.

[88] *CD* II/2, p. 99.

is really *temporal* existence. As he who 'by nature is God',[89] the *man* Jesus is in the beginning with God. In this way he *corresponds* as elected man to the electing God and in oneness with the Son of God 'not in *abstracto*, but in *concreto*, he is Jesus Christ'.[90]

One question – precisely on account of its own stringency – facing this resulting Christological interpretation of predestination is not to be suppressed: If election in Jesus Christ is really to be understood as history between God and man, must not then *faith*, too, be spoken of along with the being of the man Jesus in the beginning with God? If the election of Jesus Christ is understood as an act of the divine life of the *Spirit*, must not then faith as the work of the Holy Spirit also be spoken of along with the election of Jesus Christ? If Jesus Christ, who is already in the beginning with God as 'the authentic witness of the mercy (in which God in choosing man

---

[89] *CD* II/2, p. 96.

[90] *CD* II/2, p. 98; Barth's teaching concerning the being of the man Jesus in the beginning with God is indeed the Christological counterpart to the *theologia naturalis* which he constantly and radically rejected. Whereas Barth constantly denied a priority of God's being in the beginning with man in the creation over against revelation (which is to be understood only Christologically), Barth now teaches, on the basis of the priority of revelation (of the covenant) – which he constantly maintained – over against the creation, the being of one man in the beginning with God, which precedes the creation, i.e. the being of the elected man Jesus. With this viewpoint Barth has to a certain degree surpassed Christologically the conception of all natural theology. One will scarcely be able to make the reproach against him, that with his rejection of every natural theology he also withheld from man the theological significance which is man's due. At the same time Barth's teaching of the being of the man Jesus in the beginning with God may certainly also be understood as the Reformed counterpart to the Lutheran teaching of the participation of the human nature of Jesus Christ in the omnipresence of the *logos incarnatus*. Cf. *CD* IV/2, p. 81, where Barth describes it as highly equivocal to speak of 'a divinisation of human essence in Jesus Christ', and instead of this brings the doctrine of the *communicatio gratiarum*, which includes the rightful concern of the doctrine of the *communicatio idiomatum*, to its rightful place as pointer to the 'fullness of the concretion' which in the '*movement* made *towards* human essence' is God's 'event' (p. 84f.). If that Christological aphorism is grounded in the Lutheran doctrine of reconciliation, this Reformed aphorism springs from the doctrine of predestination. Here and there it is a question of aphorisms. One must find out what has gone missing when one breaks off the point of the Lutheran theology there, and of the Reformed theology here.

for fellowship with himself turns towards him his own glory'), is 'the original pattern of the believer',[91] must we not then also speak of the being-with-God-at-the-beginning of Jesus Christ, who grants faith through the Spirit? Is not the danger of the *decretum absolutum* only really banished in favour of a *decretum concretum* when the faith which *comes* to man is spoken of along with the election of Jesus Christ (while then in the doctrine of *reconciliation* faith as the faith which *has come* to man (cf. Gal. 3. 25) must be thematic)? This would not have to take place in the sense of the Lutheran doctrine of the *fides praevisa* – rejected by Barth[92] – which would compel predestination to be understood as *pars providentiae*. But may we not 'take in all seriousness this deriving of *praevisa fides* from the grace of the Holy Spirit and therefore from the will of God'?[93] In that case God's 'being-in-act' would be understood as being already present in the election of Jesus Christ, as a being in the act of the Spirit who makes faith possible. In precisely this way a Pelagian understanding of faith would be prevented. And this would also safeguard the fact that God's being – for the elected man, too – is a being-in-becoming.[94]

(c) God's passion

God's being-in-act becomes manifest in the temporal history of Jesus Christ. The temporal history of Jesus Christ is the temporal fulfilment of God's eternal resolve. The temporal fulfilment of God's eternal resolve is the existence of God as man in Jesus Christ. God's existence as man is not only God's existence as creature, but at the same time God's surrender of himself to the opposition to God which characterises human existence. The consequence of this self-surrender of God is God's *suffering* of his opposition which is directed against human existence in opposition to God – a suffering even to *death* on the Cross.

[91] *CD* II/2, p. 198.   [92] *CD* II/2, p. 72f.   [93] *CD* II/2, p. 73f.
[94] This critical inquiry goes back to a paper which Herr Wolfgang Hering contributed in my seminar held in the summer semester of 1963, on Barth's doctrine of election.

In this sense also, God's being is in becoming. It is a being-in-a-*becoming* threatened by *perishing*. For man in opposition to God is condemned to perish. And God suffers just this judgment in the existence of Jesus Christ. 'The more seriously we take this, the stronger becomes the temptation to approximate to the view of a contradiction and conflict in God himself.'[95] Barth takes the 'Passion of God' extremely seriously. 'The Almighty exists and acts and speaks here in the form of one who is weak and impotent, the eternal as One who is temporal and perishing . . . Here the One who lives for ever has fallen a prey to death. The Creator is subjected to and overcome by the onslaught of that which is not.'[96] But Barth categorically rejects the consequence of a contradiction through which God would come into conflict with himself.[97] For Barth *this* consequence is blasphemy. However, Barth's denial of this consequence does *not* lead to any defusing of his discussion of the suffering of God, but rather, conversely, to a criticism of the traditional metaphysical concept of God according to which God cannot suffer without falling into conflict with his being.[98] In this criticism by Barth, Barth's opposition to every form of natural theology received perhaps its most extreme formulation. No concept of

[95] *CD* IV/1, p. 185.   [96] *CD* IV/1, p. 176.

[97] *CD* IV/1, p. 185: 'God gives himself, but he does not give himself away. He does not give up being God in becoming a creature, in becoming man. He does not cease to be God. He does not come into conflict with himself.'

[98] Cf. the discussions in Werner Elert, *Der Ausgang der altkirchlichen Christologie. Eine Untersuchung über Theodor von Pharan und seine Zeit als Einführung in die alte Dogmengeschichte* (edited by Wilhelm Maurer and Elisabeth Bergsträsser; Berlin, 1957) which require to be continued. An extremely thought-provoking 'hypothetical myth' about the *suffering being* of God is related by Hans Jonas, 'Unsterblichkeit und heutige Existenz', in *Zwischen Nichts und Ewigkeit. Drei Aufsätze zur Lehre vom Menschen* (Göttingen, 1963). In the appendix an exchange of letters between R. Bultmann and H. Jonas about this 'myth' is made public. The philosophical reflections of Wilhelm Weischedel's 'Philosophische Theologie im Schatten des Nihilismus', *EvTh* 22, 1962, p. 233f.) appear, conversely, to amount to the assertion that 'God' as the reality which plunges everything real into powerlessness is *suffered*, a suffering in which man must suffer the 'farewell' from God 'in the gesture of resignation' (*op. cit.* p. 248). In answer to this, theology will only be able to speak kerygmatically of the suffering *of God* (as a farewell which has already been taken from the loneliness of a questioning which listens for no answer).

God independent of the reality of Jesus Christ may decide what is possible and impossible for God. Rather, from what God as man in Jesus Christ is, does and suffers, we learn that 'God *can* do this'.[99] For 'who God is and what it is to be divine is something we have to learn where God has revealed himself and his nature, the essence of the divine. . . . It is not for us to speak profoundly of the contradiction and rift in the being of God, but to learn to correct our notions of the being of God, to reconstitute them in the light of the fact that he *does* this. We may believe that God can and must only be absolute in contrast to all that is relative, exalted in contrast to all that is lowly, active in contrast to all suffering, inviolable in contrast to all temptation, transcendent in contrast to all immanence, and therefore divine in contrast to everything human, in short, that he can and must be only the "Wholly Other". But such beliefs are shown to be quite untenable, and corrupt and pagan, by the fact that God does in fact be and do this in Jesus Christ.'[100]

Thus it in no way contradicts the determining of God's being as 'being-in-act' when suffering is predicated of God. God's suffering corresponds to his being-in-act. But God's suffering is his being-in-*act*. Thus 'from the very first' God's 'passion is to be understood as the divine *action*'.[101] It is therefore no paradox when we also speak of 'God's being-in-the-act-of-suffering'. This statement would be a paradox if God in his essence were a god incapable of suffering, as was at times maintained among the Fathers in connection with the metaphysical concept of God drawn from Greek philosophy.[102] On

[99] *CD* IV/1, p. 187.
[100] *CD* IV/1, p. 186; also p. 129 and p. 177. Cf. earlier *CD* I/2, p. 31: 'Not only what is impossible with us men, but also what must rightly appear to us impossible with God himself, is possible with God', and certainly in so far as it has become reality to us. Cf. also *CD* IV/2, p. 92f. With the help of a presupposed philosophical concept of God 'the pride of man' denied the ontological implication of the passion of God, since according to that concept of God, 'God was far too exalted for . . . his incarnation . . . to mean anything at all for himself, or in any way to affect his Godhead.'
[101] *CD* IV/1, p. 254.
[102] Cf. the interesting expositions of Werner Elert on the apathy-axiom in the Christology of the Fathers, above all *op. cit.* p. 132.

the basis of the Barthian inference from God's being revealed to his 'inner' being, we shall have to understand, *in* God himself too, God's 'being-in-act' as a – in a certain sense – *passive* being (passive in the sense of obedience), which at the same time corresponds to the passion of the Son of God. This passivity of obedience in God is also highest activity in so far as it is *affirmed* passivity. It belongs 'to the inner *life* [my italics] of God that there should take place within it *obedience*'.[103] In the obedience of the Son of God to the Father the oneness of the being of God is not set in jeopardy through an inferiority of the Son with respect to the Father,[104] but the oneness of the divine being is *concrete* precisely indeed in its 'modes of being which are not to be separated, which are not to be regarded as autonomous, but which in their differentiation cannot be dispensed with either. He is God in their concrete relationships the one to the other, in the history which takes place between them.'[105]

The oneness of being in which God 'in himself is both One who is obeyed and Another who obeys'[106] differentiates God's 'being-in-act' from a being to be understood as 'a divine death'.[107] Just because obedience from eternity is not strange to the being of God and just because this being is everything else but 'a 'divine death', God is *able* to suffer and die as man. This intra-trinitarian *ability* of God must not, however, be thought of as a transcendental condition for the possibility of the passion of God in Jesus Christ.[108] But God's ability signifies that God is *Lord*. 'The image, the correspondence of the lordship of God, in which he has set it up and revealed it among us, for our salvation, for the reconciliation of the world with God, is, however, his obedience experienced in humility.'[109]

[103] *CD* IV/1, p. 201.
[104] For the being of God, subordination signifies no inferiority, no deficiency and no lack. Correspondingly, in the realm of the created world also, subordination should not signify 'being something less'; cf. *CD* IV/1, p. 202.
[105] *CD* IV/1, p. 203.   [106] *CD* IV/1, p. 201.   [107] *CD* IV/1, p. 561.
[108] Barth's whole theology is an emphatic protest against the transcendental method of questioning in theology, as his understanding of revelation as God's *self*-interpretation shows precisely in an axiomatic way. That is also of great significance for Barth's understanding and employment of analogy.
[109] *CD* IV/1, p. 208.

God suffers in this obedience in that in Jesus Christ he exists as man. And in this obedience God exposes himself to death. For the Son of God who became man, passion and death are not a metaphysical piece of misfortune which happened to him:[110] God *chose* this 'fate'. In his passion and death he did not therefore somehow 'waive his divinity (somewhat like the emperor of Japan in 1945)', but was rather 'in such a humiliation supremely God, in this death supremely alive', so that 'he has actually maintained and revealed his deity precisely in the passion of this man as his eternal Son'.[111] And so God *as God* has declared himself identical with the crucified Jesus. Therefore one must not exclude from this suffering the Father who gave his Son unto such suffering and death. 'It is not at all the case that God has no part in the suffering of Jesus Christ even in his mode of being as the Father.'[112] 'This fatherly fellow-suffering of God' is rather 'the basis of the humiliation of his Son', in so far as God suffers in the giving of his Son 'the alien suffering of his creature, of man, whose suffering he takes upon himself in his Son'.[113] Indeed, God's fatherly fellow-suffering as 'the basis of the humiliation of his Son' is 'realized in the historical event of his crucifixion'.[114]

Thus the Father, too, participates in the passion along with the Son, and the divine oneness of God's modes of being thus shows itself in the suffering of Jesus Christ. God's being *is* a being-in-act-of-suffering. But even in suffering God's being *remains* a being-in-*act*, a being-in-*becoming*. God wills to remain by and in the historicality of his being. And just this will of God to remain by and in the *historicality* of his being causes this being to remain – even in death – a being-in-*becoming*. In his self-surrender God does not abandon himself. But he surrenders himself because he will not abandon man. The Son of God who united himself with the Son of man, the Son of God as man, is

---

[110] 'Is the parting only for a short time
    I still feel deeply the misfortune.'
complains the widow of a cook at the royal court in Prussia in words found on her husband's gravestone in Berlin.

[111] *CD* IV/1, pp. 246–7.   [112] *CD* IV/2, p. 357.
[113] *CD* IV/2, p. 357.   [114] *CD* IV/2, p. 357.

certainly *dead*. This dead man cannot make himself alive.
Barth thinks strictly anti-docetically here. That God's being
remains a being-in-becoming – even in death – is not the work of
the Son of God who died as man.[115] But God's being remains
a being-in-*act* only in the constantly new acts of *God's self-
affirmation*. Therefore, God's will to remain by and in his historicality in the face of the death of Jesus Christ is a new act
also. In the face of the death of the Son of God who died as man,
'God's being *remains* in becoming' signifies the *new*[116] act of the
resurrection which happens to the Son of God and with him the
man Jesus. In saying Yes to the dead Son of God, God said Yes
also to man, and indeed with the *same* Yes. In that *God* here
corresponds to himself anew he brings *man* also anew into a
correspondence with God. For in the resurrection of Jesus Christ
man is given a part in the being of God which prevails against
death. But this *imparting*, too, belongs as grace to God's being-
in-act. And thus it belongs to the *being* of God to *become* the God
of every man.[117]

---

[115] *CD* IV/1, p. 303f.; the death of the Son of God may not only be understood as powerlessness 'from which he recovered on his own initiative and in
his own strength' (against Heinrich Vogel, *Gott in Christo. Ein Erkenntnisgang
durch die Grundprobleme der Dogmatik*, Berlin, 1951, p. 739). The difficulties of
the traditional Christology with respect to the death of Christ were clearly
perceived by Otto Weber, *Grundlagen der Dogmatik* II (Neukirchen, 1962), p.
144f. Berkouwer (*op. cit.* p. 307), sees in the fact that Barth does 'not speak
so openly of the "death of God"', 'a conspicuous fact (a symptom of
drawing back) which cannot be perceived on the basis of Barth's premise'.

[116] Therein the Christian doctrine of God is necessarily distinguished
from such an impressive philosophical outline as that which Hans Jonas sets
forth in his 'hypothetical myth': here also the attempt is made to formulate
the historicality of God radically. But the concept of God in this 'hypothetical myth' is not the Christian concept. God's being is thus not formulated in a Trinitarian manner. It is strictly logical when the historicality of
this 'God' becomes concrete in his 'self-denial', following which no *new* act
of God can take place: 'After he gave himself completely to the world in its
becoming, God has nothing more to give: now it is man's turn to give to
him' (*Zwischen Nichts und Ewigkeit*, p. 60).

[117] The fact that God's being is a being *pro nobis* which brings him to be
present *in nobis* is founded on the historicality of God's *extra nos esse*. Cf. K.
Barth, 'Extra nos – pro nobis – in nobis', in: *Hören und Handeln, Festschrift
für Ernst Wolf* (Munich, 1962), p. 15f.

(d) God's being is in becoming

At the end of this paraphrase we shall briefly confront Barth's
exposition of God's being with Gollwitzer's exposition of God's
existence as confessed by faith. On the one hand the confrontation will be restricted to the difficulty in Gollwitzer's book
which remained unsolved and which may be formulated in
the following question: How is God's being-in-and-for-itself,
maintained by Gollwitzer, related to God's being-for-us which
is also maintained by Gollwitzer and which provided the basis
for the assertion of God's being-in-and-for-itself? On the other
hand the confrontation will be in the form of a summary –
certainly a rather sketchy one – of the preceding paraphrase.
Thereby the same problem will be discussed in its various
aspects, so that there will necessarily be repetitions.

Gollwitzer maintained that we must not 'evade or shrink
from saying: '*God is in-and-for-himself.*'[118] This proposition should
be understood not 'as a speculative proposition' but rather as
the expression for 'an indispensable element in the knowledge
of faith'.[119] For the aim of the proposition is to prevent the
being of God being identified with God's being-for-us, so that
this fact shall be firmly established: 'in God's being-for-us man
receives a free, unmerited gift . . . which is not based upon
anything that is necessary to God . . .'.[120]

Expressed in the concepts of classical ontology this means
that God, as he who exists concretely, is a first substance. For
it is a characteristic of the so-called first substances that as such
they are not necessarily related to something other. First substances are as such no relation towards something [πρός τι] and
certainly they are to be comprehended as relational being
neither as wholes, nor with respect to their parts: ἐπὶ μὲν γὰρ τῶν
πρώτων οὐσιῶν ἀληθές ἐστι · οὔτε γὰρ τὰ ὅλα οὔτε τὰ μέρη πρός τι
λέγεται.[121] If on the other hand one would wish to comprehend

[118] *The Existence of God*, p. 217.   [119] *Ibid.* p. 217.   [120] *Ibid.* p. 217.
[121] So in Categories 8a 15f., a writing attributed to Aristotle but whose
genuineness is regarded as doubtful; if it is genuine it must be one of
Aristotle's earliest writings.

God in his being as relational being, then the being of the other
to which God in his being were to be related would necessarily
be connoted with the being of God. For all relational being so
far as it is specified according to its own peculiarity demands
the other to which it is related, reciprocally: πάντα οὖν τὰ πρός
τι, ἐάνπερ οἰκείως ἀποδιδῶται, πρὸς ἀντιστρέφοντα λέγεται.[122] Thus
if one would wish to comprehend God's being as such under the
category of relational being and if one would have to regard
man as the something other to which God as God is related,
then God without man could not be comprehended as God;
likewise, but conversely, God would then also have to be always
connoted with the concept[123] of man. Gollwitzer wants to
prevent just that.[124] Now it shall certainly not be denied that
God has *turned* himself *towards* man, that he *is* really *for us*. That
God's being is *also* relational being is for Gollwitzer not in
question. But this relationship of God to man is not a necessary
attribute of God's being. Rather is God's relationship to man a
contingent relation which must not make God's being-in-and-
for-itself into a problem. God in his determining as God is not
then related necessarily (πρὸς αὐτὸ ὃ λέγεται) to man but only
ἐάν γε πρὸς τὸ τυχὸν[125] ἀποδιδῶται, that is, contingently. And
just for this reason God and man do not make demands on each
other reciprocally, for if it refers to what is contingent – not to
what is necessary – the relationship is not reciprocal (ἐπεὶ ἐάν γε
πρὸς τὸ τυχὸν ἀποδιδῶται καὶ μὴ πρὸς αὐτὸ ὃ λέγεται, οὐκ
ἀντιστρέφει).[126]

Gollwitzer thus comprehends God's being completely in the

---

[122] *Cat.* 7a 22f.

[123] In the strict meaning of the expression λόγος τῆς οὐσίας.

[124] Cf. Wilfried Joest, 'Die Personalität des Glaubens', *KuD* 7, 1961, p.
152: God 'does not become in the human Thou, but he is'. See also Gotthold
Hasenhüttl: 'As much as one can agree with what has been said, there is
still in my opinion too much proven' (G. Hasenhüttl, *Der Glaubensvollzug.
Eine Begegnung mit Rudolf Bultmann aus katholischem Glaubensverständnis,
Koinonia, Beiträge zur ökumenischen Spiritualität und Theologie*, Essen, 1963,
p. 320).

[125] Whereby for Gollwitzer (in distinction from Aristotle) the πρὸς τὸ
τυχόν according to which God's being would be here determined must be
the consequence of a divine resolve.　　　　　[126] *Cat.* 7a 23f.

sense of the classical concept of substance.[127] However, he does not consciously make use of this concept. For Gollwitzer the essential thing is to comprehend God's being as person-being. 'The personal way of speaking is unsurpassable for Christian talk of God.'[128] But: 'Personal being means being in relationship!'[129] And: 'It must therefore be emphatically maintained that person is a concept expressing relationship, or at any rate it may be used theologically only (!) as a concept of relationship and not as a concept of substance expressing the nature of *a magnitude existing for itself*.'[130] On the other hand, however, 'we must not evade or shrink from saying: God is in-and-for-himself'.[131]

The dilemma which originates here is plain. Gollwitzer resists it 'through the distinction between a God's being-for-us which flows from the freedom of his being-for-himself, and a being-for-our-sake in which God is only thought of in a functional sense, since he cannot like worldly entities be demonstrated in objective independence.'[132] Thus God is not to be thought of 'only in a functional sense', although God's being can be comprehended only as 'personal being', and 'personal being' according to Gollwitzer 'may be used, at any rate theologically, only as a concept of relationship'. Gollwitzer's explications compel a clarification of the relation-concept with whose help it is supposed to be possible for God's being to be formulated adequately.

If God's 'being-for-us' is not to be a 'being-for-our sake' then

---

[127] In Aristotle the 'classical concept of substance' is offered in the category of οὐσία. But what is later a more current and thus a classical terminus is in Aristotle still *an attempt at reflection*. The concept of οὐσία in the *Categories* is by no means already polished, but rather (pre-supposing the early dating of the writing) a *first* attempt to demarcate the boundary with Plato (namely the attempt to comprehend presence primarily as object [that-ness] and only secondarily as quality [what-ness]); after this further attempts will follow, as *Metaphysics* Z, above all, shows. Cf. Martin Heidegger, *Nietzsche*, vol. II (Pfullingen, 1961), pp. 399–410; Ernst Tugendhat, TI KATA TINOΣ. *Eine Untersuchung zu Struktur und Ursprung aristotelischer Grundbegriffe*, Symposion 2 (Freiburg-Munich, 1958).

[128] *The Existence of God*, p. 188.
[129] *Ibid*. p. 188.
[130] *Ibid*. p. 187 (my italics).
[131] *Ibid*. p. 217.
[132] *Ibid*. p. 232.

it must be asked how God's being-for-us *can* be thought of as a relation without God being thought of 'only in a functional sense'. If one concedes the necessity of this distinction then the inquiry into the *relation* between God's being-for-us and the freedom of his being-for-himself becomes even more pressing. One should not be deceived: if this *relation* is not comprehended, then revelation as revelation remains uncomprehended. The reference to God's 'groundless mercy'[133] can here, therefore, not be the last word, because it has significance theologically only in so far as it excludes a ground for God's mercy 'external' to God himself.[134] However, if God's unfathomable mercy must not have its ground in God's *being*, then the concept of mercy is no longer a concept of God. Gollwitzer has no inkling of this consequence. But does he avoid it when he clings to his distinction between God's essence and God's will?[135]

It is clear that this distinction of Gollwitzer's is also meant in an anti-metaphysical sense. But is not a metaphysical background introduced into God's being precisely through this distinction, which will permit as theologically legitimate only speech about the essence of the will of God? Is not Gollwitzer prevented from thinking of God's being in a consistent historical way precisely because of this distinction and demarcation? Must not the very *freedom* of God's being-for-himself be *formulated* starting from the *grace* of God's being-for-us which has been revealed, and indeed, so that God's being can become event in the grace of God's being-for-us because God's being in the freedom of his being-for-himself is originally event?

Whoever, like Gollwitzer, wants to maintain and think of God's independence cannot avoid the task of conceiving God's independence (*Selbständigkeit*) *out of* God's own subsistence (*Selbstand*) and thus also of thinking of *this subsistence*. God's subsistence is certainly to be thought of *only* out of God's revelation, thus out of an event in which God's being has become manifest as being-for-us. But then one will not be able to think of God's being as subsistence in the sense in which

133 *Ibid.* p. 217.   134 Cf. *CD* IV/1, p. 184.
135 *The Existence of God*, p. 186.

Plato conceives essence (οὐσία), to which he ascribes the definition of 'being' (λόγος τοῦ εἶναι): are these essences . . . always
what they are, having the same simple self-existent and un-
changing forms, not admitting of variation at all, or in any
way, or at any time? (ἀεὶ . . . ὃ ἔστι, μονοειδὲς ὃν αὐτὸ καθ᾽ αὑτό
(translated as 'in-and-for-itself' by Schleiermacher!), ὡσαύτως
καὶ κατὰ ταὐτὰ ἔχει καὶ οὐδέποτε οὐδαμῇ οὐδαμῶς ἀλλοίωσιν οὐδεμίαν
ἐνδέχεται).[136] Such a being as subsistence excludes the *event* out
of itself, so that such an independent being cannot reveal
itself. The subsistence of being as idea excludes the event of
revelation because it excludes the *event* of being as subsistence.
'God is in-and-for-himself' therefore remains an extremely
mistaken statement so long as the independence of God which
is maintained in this statement is not formulated out of the
event of revelation, such that thereby God's being as subsistence
allows the event of revelation to be formulated from this being.

But if God's being as subsistence is so thought of, that this
being makes the event of revelation not impossible, but first and
foremost possible, then the being of God as subsistence which is
deduced from the event of God's revelation is itself thought of
as event. And, indeed, as an event *granting* the event of revelation. God's independent being must thus be understood from the
event of revelation as an event granting this event of revelation.
God's being as subsistence is self-movement. As self-movement
God's independent being makes revelation possible. Revelation
as God's interpretation of himself is the expression of this self-
movement of the being of God. Formulated differently: The
grace of God's being-for-us must be able to be a 'copy' (*Abbild*)
of the freedom of God's being-for-himself, so that this freedom
as the 'original' (*Urbild*) of that grace becomes visible in that

---

[136] *Phaedo* 78d. In distinction from Plato Barth differentiates the concept
of the divine being in such a way that he can think of this being likewise as
self-subsistence *and* as event: God can be other without becoming another.
'In himself he is quite different from what he is in our own work (i.e. the
knowledge of God). . . . Yet while this is true, it is also true that both in
himself and in our work he is not Another' (*CD* II/1, p. 227). Without a leap
into another category (μετάβασις εἰς ἄλλο γένος) he is, *in another way, the
same* for us as he is for himself.

grace as the 'copy' of this freedom. If revelation as God's *being-for-us* is to be taken seriously, then in Jesus Christ God's being must *become* visible and *be able* to become visible. This means, however, that both this becoming as well as this being-able to become must be understood from God's being itself, if indeed it is really true that *God* has revealed *himself*. Thus the historicality of God must be formulated *from God*. And on the other side, God's being must be formulated in view of this becoming and of this being-able to become if indeed it is really true that God has *revealed* himself. Thus at all cost we must formulate God's *historicality*.

Yet what help is the assurance that one must speak of God's being historically, when one *cannot* speak historically of God's being? It is still not achieved by ascribing historical predicates to the concept of God. History and the being of God are then again all too easily caused to be divided from one another. God's being is first then and only then really formulated historically when God's being as such is comprehended as historical being.

In such comprehension, however, the all important thing is that history does not in any way become a general concept for the being of God. 'God's being is historical' is and must remain a proposition of revelation. As a proposition of revelation this proposition is itself certainly an historical proposition. For revelation is an historical event or it is just not revelation. But revelation is just that historical event in which God's being shows itself as a being which is not only able to bear historical predicates, but demands them! In the historical event of revelation God's being is itself event, and indeed with the result that *human* language (and thus 'anthropomorphic' language also; for human language even as the most abstract language – certainly hidden from itself – is 'anthropomorphic'[137]) about God becomes not only appropriate, but necessary.[138]

This necessity does not veil the fact, but makes it first and foremost manifest, that human speech as such is not suited

---

[137] Cf. Bruno Snell, *Die Entdeckung des Geistes* (3rd ed.; Hamburg, 1955).
[138] Gollwitzer has shown this well, *op. cit.* pp. 142–201.

to speak about God. The demand made by God's being for historical predicates does not cover, but first and foremost un-covers, the fact that historical predicates are as such not suited to predicate the being of God. But if, however, it is true that the being of God must not only be spoken about historically, but also can be spoken about, then God's being must be historical in a more original way than historical predicates are historical.[139]

Barth's understanding of revelation as God's self-interpreta-tion is the systematic attempt to think of God's being-in-itself as event in such a way that God's being is capable of possessing historical predicates, although these as such are not capable of predicating the being of God. In that God in revelation *inter-prets* himself, God's being is *reiterated* with the help of historical predicates. Since, however, this self-interpretation is a re-iteration *of the being of God through God,* God's being as such is a being capable of reiteration. As being capable of reiteration, God's being is *event.* For being which is no event can only 'reiterate' itself as tautological identity. God's revelation, however, is not tautological identity, but indeed *self-interpreta-tion.*

At this point a further reflection is indispensable: this first enables us to comprehend fully that God's being is not only able to bear historical predicates – in spite of their unqualified nature – but also demands them. For if it is true that God's being on the basis of the reiteration of this being which has taken place as revelation is a being capable of reiteration, then it will also have to be true that God's being on the basis of the self-interpretation of this being which has taken place as revela-tion is a being capable of interpretation. Take note: capable of being reiterated and interpreted by God alone. But just this, too, must be understood – that from eternity God is capable of interpreting himself through himself. The ability to possess

---

[139] If one does not think of God's being on the ground of his revelation as historical being already in itself, then it is now, conversely, only a short step to the consequence of thinking of history as revelation, or as God's becoming. And it is then just a short step to let the renewal of faith be founded on 'historical facts' as such, a procedure which according to Wilhelm Herr-mann is known to be unethical.

H

predicates must belong constitutively to God's historicality. The *ability* to possess predicates, however, is the *event of the word* which is there before all predications and which makes all predications possible. In this sense it will have to be true that God's being, which has been formulated from the event of revelation, is in himself *verbal* (*wörtlich*) and precisely in this same measure also historical. That the logos is in the beginning with God – if this logos is supposed to be the subject of the historical predicate 'Jesus of Nazareth' – is of intratrinitarian relevance.

How are we to understand the assertion that God's being is verbal in himself? God's being is verbal in himself in so far as God says 'Yes' to himself. This 'Yes' of God to himself constitutes his being as God the Father, God the Son and God the Holy Spirit. And at the same time, from the beginning, this constitutes the historicality of God's being, in which all history has its basis. This 'Yes' of God to himself is the *mystery* of God's being and as such one cannot go behind it. For in God's 'saying Yes' to himself, God's being *corresponds* to itself as Father, as Son and as Holy Spirit. This correspondence is an absolute mystery and cannot be surpassed by any paradox.

In this correspondence the being of God takes place as the history of the divine life in the Spirit. And in the history which is constituted through this correspondence God *makes space* within himself for *time*. This making-space-for-time within God is a continuing event. This space of time which is so comprehended as a continuing event we call eternity. 'God has time, because and as he has eternity.'[140] 'We know eternity primarily and properly not by the negation of the concept of time. . . . The theological concept of eternity must be set free from the Babylonian captivity of an abstract opposite to the concept of time.'[141] This takes place when eternity is comprehended as the continuing event[142] of the making-space-for-

---

[140] *CD* II/1, p. 611.   [141] *CD* II/1, p. 611.

[142] God's '*stare* is also a *fluere*, but without the instability which belongs to all creaturely *fluere*, the *fluere* of empirical time. Again, his *fluere* is also a *stare*, but without the immutability that belongs to all creaturely *stare*, the *stare* which is proper to the various times as they become a problem in our reflection on them' (*ibid.*).

time, and thus as God's space of time. God *is* in this space of time in that he *goes his* ways. 'To say that God moves in certain directions is not a mere figure of speech, nor is it a reality only in his relation to what he has created. It is an eternal reality in himself.'[143]

The eternity in which God goes his ways, is, as the space of time for which God continually makes space within himself, not a-historical but in an eminent sense historical. And because God's being in eternity, which is constituted through the correspondence of Father, Son and Spirit, is historical, revelation is therefore possible as 'eternity in a single moment'. The mystery of the correspondence of his being which takes place in God's self-affirmation makes revelation as historical event possible, and in this event it becomes manifest as mystery.

Single moments do not tarry but single moments can make history. Revelation as 'eternity in a single moment' makes history, in that revelation brings human being into correspondence with the being of God which corresponds to itself. And in just this way human speech about God becomes possible in the 'freedom for the word' (Ernst Fuchs) which is granted by God. It owes its being to revelation in which God himself – and that means his being! – manifested himself in human language. The historical predicate by which God manifested his being in human language is called Jesus of Nazareth. This predicate, too, is as such not suited to act as a predicate of God's being.[144] It is as such not the predicate of an analytical proposition. What the patristic doctrine of the *anhypostasis* had to say of the human nature of Jesus Christ is true of this predicate as such. 'Jesus of Nazareth' as such cannot be regarded as a predicate of revelation.[145] But this predicate

---

[143] *CD* II/1, p. 593.

[144] In this sense the question of the historical Jesus, which has been posed anew in the school of R. Bultmann, is today easily misunderstood.

[145] That is also the position of the great Marburg teacher in questions concerning the historical Jesus, a position which Bultmann's pupils too, have not abandoned. Whether one must also draw the same consequences from this position as Bultmann himself has finally done in his Heidelberg University lecture 'Das Verhältnis der urchristlichen Christusbotschaft zum

is *true* as substantial to the word of God (ἐνυπόστατος τῷ λόγῳ τοῦ θεοῦ).[146] In order that this predicate might be true, God elected it from eternity. Is it too much to assert with Barth that the Word (λόγος), in which 'Jesus of Nazareth' alone can be the predicate of revelation, was already with God in the beginning as the subject of this historical predicate and thus 'the *locum tenens* for Jesus'? [147] With his teaching of the being of the man Jesus in the beginning with God, Barth has taught us to understand the relation of the historicality of God's being to the historical predicates Christologically. One will have to prize this theological pronouncement as something valuable so long as one has nothing better to set in its place.

In the attempt to overcome the difficulty to which we were led by Gollwitzer's book we have passed over to the interpretation of Barth's own statements. We will now have to clarify

historischen Jesus' (*Sitzungsberichte der Heidelberger Akademie der Wissenschaften, philosophisch-historische Klasse*, 3. Abhandlung, Heidelberg, 1961²) is disputable.

[146] The subject matter itself becomes plain within the proclamation of Jesus in his parables of the kingdom of God. Cf. above all Ernst Fuchs, 'Zur Frage nach dem historischen Jesus', *Gesammelte Aufsätze* II (Tübingen, 1960).

[147] The above exposition of the correspondence of God's being as the history of the divine life in the *Spirit* could provoke the question whether therewith something like a 'corporal being' of God would not be *a priori* excluded from thinking. In my opinion that must not necessarily be the case. For in so far as God makes space for time in his eternal history, one will also be able to speak of God's *corporal being*. It would consist in the assertion that God has *space* (*Raum*) in his being. Even that, certainly, makes sense only as a proposition of revelation. And thus Barth speaks directly and concretely Christologically with reference to Jn. 1. 1 of the logos as *locum tenens* for Jesus. Thus from eternity God's being has *space* for human history. In that God *makes space within himself* for time, he also makes space for us and gives us a place by himself. The exposition of God's corporeality in this sense becomes eschatologically relevant in so far as Barth understands the eschatological being of man as 'an eternal being . . . secure in God' without the difference from the eternal being of God itself being obliterated (cf. *CD* IV/1, p. 8). One could define as follows: God's corporeality is the eternal space of time which makes space for participation in God's being, a space of time which God himself makes space for in himself (cf. Jn. 14. 2). Thus God's corporeality would in fact then be the end of all the ways of God, but God's corporeality as the space of the spiritual body (σῶμα πνευματικόν) which is promised us, full of life and love.

what meaning these statements have for the formal task set us by Gollwitzer's book, the task of thinking out God's being as a relationship.

The fact that God *becomes manifest* means that God's being is relational being. But if the dilemma sketched above is now to be avoided, if God's being is to be comprehended as *in relation to something* (πρός τι) and yet to remain protected from being dependent on every *other thing* (ἕτερον) without on the other hand the relation becoming the *accidens* of a substance existing in and for itself, then one will have to understand God's being essentially as *double* relational being. This means that God can enter into relationship (*ad extra*) with another being (and just in this relationship his being can exist ontically *without* thereby being ontologically dependent on this other being), because God's being (*ad intra*) is a being *related to itself*. The doctrine of the Trinity is an attempt to think out the self-relatedness of God's being.[148] It attempts to think out the self-relatedness of the being of God as Father, Son and Spirit, but it can only do this appropriately when it understands God's self-relatedness in his modes of being (not at all as a kind of ontological egoism of God, but rather) as the *power* of God's being *to become* the God of another. It must not be made a condition that God's becoming must first take place through 'something other than God' perhaps even in the sense of a transcendental condition positing the possibility of God being our God.[149] God's self-relatedness

[148] Gollwitzer in a footnote (*op. cit.* p. 187, fn. 3) indicates the possibility of speaking in a Trinitarian way of God's self-relatedness: 'God's personal-being apart from and before his relation to us could be spoken of only in terms of the relations of the immanent Trinity, as in Barth's exposition.' Strangely enough Gollwitzer proceeds no further than this indication although only the possibility here indicated could guard against the difficulty from which Gollwitzer's book cannot now escape. Certainly Herbert Braun would let himself be convinced by the doctrine of an immanent Trinity even less than by Gollwitzer's arguments. But on the other hand I see no reason why one should give up a pressing invitation to those exegetes who employ the historical-critical method to rethink systematically and consequently the possibility of the historical-critical method within theology from the object of theology.

[149] This danger, however, threatens speech concerning God's being-in-and-for-himself!

must rather be understood as a *becoming*,[150] *peculiar*[151] to his *own* being, a becoming which allows us to comprehend God's being as a 'being-in-act'. Only when God's self-relatedness is understood as a becoming peculiar to his own being is God's being-for-us also adequately considered.[152] God's self-relatedness, his

[150] The fact that God's being is in becoming constitutes eternity as temporality in sense of the being in-one-another and by-one-another of the three modes of time. Thus the becoming proper to God's being is not constituted by temporality, but temporality is constituted by the becoming.

[151] If one takes account of the fact that God's being in becoming is a becoming *proper* to this being, then one will not be able to make distinctions between God's existentiality (*Existentialität*) and its 'concrete actualizations' (*Aktualisierungen*) as Schubert M. Ogden following the philosophy of Charles Hartshorne recommends us to do: 'Zur Frage der "richtigen" Philosophie', *ZThK* 61 (1964), p. 103f. According to Schubert M. Ogden the existentiality of God, which is to be distinguished from God's existence, is 'the abstract structure or form of his essence which characterizes him as God and distinguishes him from all other essences' (*op. cit.* p. 119). This existentiality of God is 'the ground of each concrete actualization' (*ibid.* p. 119). Existentiality and concrete actualization are related as two 'poles' of the divine being. In the one ' "pole" of his being God is eminent subject which transcends the conceptual analysis' (*ibid.* p. 118). The other 'pole' of the divine being is its existentiality which therewith becomes the object of a 'phenomenology of the divine being' (*ibid.* p. 121). Thus Heidegger's fundamental-ontological distinction between 'ontic' and 'ontological', between '*existentiell*' and '*existential*' is carried over on to the being of God. Characteristic of this is the statement of Hartshorne (whose works at the present time here in East Berlin are unfortunately not accessible to me) cited by Ogden: 'Philosophy seeks that general principle or essence of the divine being of which such concrete actions of God are mere contingent illustrations' (*ibid.* p. 117; from Hartshorne's, *The Divine Relativity*, New Haven, 1948, p. xii).

It is clear that Barth's concept of Trinitarian theology cannot well be brought into agreement with such a 'phenomenology of the divine being'. In Barth's exposition it is a question of understanding 'the other "pole" of the divine being', too, as God's being in *becoming*. God's being cannot become thematic in abstraction from the becoming proper to this being, just as, conversely, this becoming can be understood neither 'solely as . . . contingent illustration' of the divine being nor at all as a becoming different from God's being. God's being is as such concrete – that is the point of the Christian doctrine of the Trinity which precisely forbids a 'phenomenology of the divine being'. Rudolf Bultmann may, at least in this negation, stand nearer to Karl Barth than to any philosopher. Cf. Bultmann's attitude to Schubert M. Ogden: 'Zur Frage einer "philosophischen Theologie" ', in: *Einsichten. Gerhard Krüger zum 60. Geburtstag* (Frankfurt/Main, 1962), p. 36f.

[152] So long as the becoming in which God's being is, is understood as the

power to be in relation to himself (εἶναι πρὸς ἑαυτόν), would
then be the power of his being in relation to another (πρὸς
ἕτερον). God's eternal love in which Father, Son and Holy
Spirit become eternally one would then be the ground (with
respect to all that is not God) of his groundless mercy. God's
being in relation to another (πρὸς ἕτερον) is thus no farewell to
himself. God's being-for-us is just as little farewell to himself as
it is God's coming-to-himself.[153]

Thus it is not enough to formulate God's being simply as
a being in relationship. A conscious or unconscious natural
theology certainly does not become Protestant by making the
relation the basic category of its statements. And the relation as
'pure relationship' is still not formulated adequately enough so
long as this its purity is not formulated theologically.[154]

---

becoming *proper* to God's being, the statement 'God's being is in becoming'
remains from the first guarded from the misunderstanding that God *would*
first *become* that which he is, through his relationship to an other than
himself. God therefore does not first become in the faith which he grants.
But certainly God chooses to become in faith what he *already is*. And in so
far God, in the self-relatedness of his being in becoming, is already ours in
advance. Karl Barth may have sharpened in a Trinitarian way Luther's
statement about God's becoming (*fieri*). For Luther, cf. Rudolf Hermann,
'Das Verhältnis von Rechtfertigung und Gebet', in: *Gesammelte Studien zur
Theologie Luthers und der Reformation* (Göttingen, 1960), p. 16f., fn. 14. With
regard to the problem of God's becoming cf. Rahner, 'On the Theology of
the Incarnation', in: *Theological Investigations IV*, pp. 105–20, and G.
Hasenhüttl, *op. cit.* p. 321f.

[153] According to Barth this last statement would be true with respect to
Hegel. Cf. *Die protestantische Theologie im 19. Jahrhundert* (Zürich-Zollikon
1952²), p. 377; ET, *Protestant Theology in the Nineteenth Century* (London,
1972), p. 420. 'The Church is necessary to God himself, for in it he can be
the mind of the Church; and it is this alone which first makes it possible for
him to be mind and God. If he were not the mind of the Church he would
not be God. And he is God only in so far as he is the mind of the Church.
I am necessary to God. That is the basis of Hegel's confidence in God, and
the reason why this confidence can immediately and without further ado be
understood as self-confidence as well, and why it did thus understand
itself.' Cf. also Hegel's *Lectures on the Philosophy of Religion* (London, 1895) I,
p. 200: 'Without the world God is not God.'

[154] Is then the purity of the relationship *philosophically* formulated when
the relationship is formulated from out of itself, as the later Heidegger
obviously attempts to do? Cf. most recently: *Die Technik und die Kehre*
(Pfullingen, 1962).

Protestant theology cannot formulate the purity of the relationship without an origin of relationship, which as the origin of the relationship *is*, in that it *sets itself in relation*. Such setting-itself-in-relation is, understood theologically, pure relationship. And in the sense of such a setting-itself-in-relation God's being is *essentially relational*; God's being is 'pure relationship'.

Pure relationship thus means relationship as a becoming of itself but not from itself.[155] But then from what does it become? God's self-relatedness is based on God's 'Yes' to himself. In this 'Yes' of God to himself God sets himself in relation to himself, in order so to be he who he is. In this sense God's being is in becoming. 'Pure relationship' can thus be only the predicate,

[155] 'Pure relationship' thought of in another sense than this threatens in its purity to become relationless. We have, therefore, also in the Trinitarian being of God, to do with 'pure relationships' in no other sense than that of origin-relations in which God as Father is the eternal origin of the Son and with the Son the eternal origin of the Spirit. *In* these origin-relations God is who he is. One must therefore not confuse the statement 'God's being is in becoming' with other statements such as: God's being is becoming, or: God's being becomes in becoming.

Heinrich Vogel (likewise led by the concern to express God's being as concrete being) has interpreted God's I-being as act-being and sought to understand *theologically* the *purity* of God's act-being out of God's being-for-us, which becomes manifest in the event of the resurrection of he-who-died-for-us. 'How shall we now wish to understand that which eventuates there in the mystery of his resurrection other than as pure act!' (*op. cit.* p. 322). 'Pure act' is thereby, according to Vogel, 'not a *neutral* event which would somehow be able to be separated from the divine *subject* as it reveals itself in this happening' (*ibid.* p. 321). God himself as the being in this happening is rather '*actus purus*, pure act' (*ibid.* p. 322). Vogel then defines God's act-being through the *relations* of God's out-of-itself-being and God's being-for-itself and being-for-others. Thus in Vogel we run up against the same problem with which we sought to grapple by employing the proposition 'God's being is in becoming'. What 'becoming' means here is in fact to be understood Christologically, and the legitimate foundation of such a Christological understanding will in fact be the event of the resurrection of Jesus from the dead. Here it is a question of a becoming whose subject is God and only God and which is, at the same time, the ontological place of the being of God's Son who died for us. It will hardly require to be pointed out that the being of the God 'who did not become' can certainly be *in becoming*, indeed that only a being which *is* in becoming is really properly being which has not become.

but never the subject of a proposition related to God. But this predicate can be the predicate of an analytical and a synthetic proposition. With respect to God's Trinitarian self-relatedness this predicate is to be understood as that of an analytical proposition. With respect to God's revelation this predicate is to be understood as that of a synthetic proposition. The synthetic proposition nevertheless *corresponds* to the analytical proposition. This correspondence signifies that God's being as self-relatedness is a being in becoming, which possesses the peculiarity of being able to *reiterate itself*.[156]

The reiteration, however, is nothing without that which is to be reiterated. That means in Gollwitzer's sense that God's being-for-us is nothing without God's being-for-himself. The *ratio essendi* of the reiteration is that which is to be reiterated. The problems which become thematic in this context must be considered as a counterpart to the doctrines of *enhypostasis* and *anhypostasis* in a doctrine of the reiteration of God's being. For if God's being for us is the reiteration of his being for himself, such a doctrine of reiteration would have to bring to its rightful

---

[156] To 'reiterate itself' is something other than to 'reiterate something'. Because God in revelation does not reiterate *something* but reiterates *himself*, 'faith, therefore, also understands revelation not as *something* new, but understands it only in that it understands *itself* anew in revelation' (Bultmann, *Glauben und Verstehen* I, p. 297; ET, *Faith and Understanding* I, London, 1969, p. 316). Gollwitzer's concern that Bultmann could have forgotten 'that in faith man understands God also anew and that revelation brings him "something new" inasmuch as he did not know God before as the One who is God, but is now confronted by God himself' (*The Existence of God*, p. 34) may have already been adequately allayed by Bultmann himself three pages before and six pages after the sentence quoted by Gollwitzer. 'But faith speaks of God as other than the world. Faith knows that God becomes manifest only through his revelation and that in the light of that revelation everything which was previously called God is not God' (*Faith and Understanding*, pp. 313–14). 'It therefore remains true that all human speaking of God apart from faith speaks not of God, but of the devil' (*Faith and Understanding*, p. 322). Can one actually say it more plainly? In face of the apprehension which is continually being heard, that for Bultmann 'God's being is identical with the word-event in which it arises and is exhausted' (*The Existence of God*, p. 34), we may be reminded that Bultmann is one of the theologians who saw through and expressly rejected natural theology as an undertaking whose aim was 'to eliminate God as the "Beyond" and "Other worldly" in relation to man' (*Faith and Understanding*, p. 314).

place with respect to the relations, that which the doctrines of *enhypostasis* and *anhypostasis* seek to validate christologically for the poles of the relation (God – man). Thereby the doctrine of *anhypostasis* would now be formulated together with that of *enhypostasis* by opposing the two doctrines to each other: God's being *ad extra* would be anhypostatic if in this relation an *enhypostasis* of the being of God as Father, as Son and as Spirit was not fulfilled. But in that God in his revelation reiterates his being as Father, as Son, and as Spirit as being for us, this re-iteration also possesses being. This would mean that God in his revelation *imparts* himself to his concrete relational existence as Father, Son, and Spirit by reiterating himself. The reiteration as God's relation to us is the correspondence to God's self-relatedness: *analogia relationis*.[157] Revelation, so understood, is really God's self-interpretation. And so understood, God in his revelation can *be* πρὸς ἕτερον without being dependent upon this ἕτερον. But conversely, man and his world owe their being to the being of God πρὸς ἕτερον. In the irreversibility of this ontological relatedness of God and the world lies the ontological difference between God and the world. Hence God can be the God of man without being defined as God by a relation to man. Yet at the same time, if the proposition concerning the reitera-tion of God's being in the correspondence of the relations *ad extra* and *ad intra* is really true, the proposition 'God is in-and-for-himself' *in concreto* is just as false as the proposition 'God is God only as the God of man'.[158]

[157] Cf. *CD* IV/1, p. 186: 'As God was in Christ, far from being against himself, or at disunity with himself, . . . he has done that which corresponds to his divine nature.' 'Between the two, i.e. between the relationship in God himself and God's relationship to the world, there is an obvious proportion' (*CD* III/1, p. 49). The analogy of relations is thus an *analogia proportionalitatis*. For my criticism of the Catholic interpretation of this use of analogy in Barth's writings, carried on through Hans Urs von Balthasar and Gottlieb Söhngen, cf. my article in *EvTh* 22, 1962, p. 535f.

[158] Gollwitzer certainly wanted to express this point by speaking of the necessity and unsuitability of is-propositions with respect to God's being. But the proposition 'God is in-and-for-himself' is an unsuitable proposition not only with respect to all worldly being, but all the more and most of all with respect to God's being, so long as it is not derived from the *analogia relationis*. But if it is the correspondence of relations, then it is all the more an

What has been said may be summed up as follows:

1. What may be known and said about God's being may only be known and stated from God's being-for-us.

---

unsuitable proposition in which a negatively disguised soteriological interest is hidden. This proposition is not free from the suspicion that in it – quite against Gollwitzer's intentions – the theology of consciousness has been turned upside down. As such it would certainly also remain a theology of consciousness. One will, therefore, have to bring forward Iwand's protest against the misuse of the *pro me* as a methodological principle in theology (cf. *EvTh*, 1954, p. 120f.) with the same stringency and sharpness against the misuse found in the theory of knowledge of a 'God in himself' as methodological principle in theology. That 'we do not have to reckon . . . with any Son of God *in himself*' (*CD* IV/1, p. 52), can only confirm the rejection of talk about 'God's being-in-and-for-itself'. We should here remember Hermann Cremer's circumspect undertaking to consider in a theologically appropriate way God's essence and act, God's revelation and his differentiation from us in his revelation: 'Therefore God's actions belong to his essence, and the determination of his actions by his essence yields his attributes in which the distinction between God and us, between God and those to whom he relates himself permeates all the relationships which are firmly set through the fact of this relation. The attributes of God are thus God's differentiation from us which manifests itself for us and to us in all relationships which this relation to us brings with it, the determination of his appearance in his actions through his essence. When, however, the actions and the essence of God so belong together that the former is the consummated manifestation of his essence, then the attributes are attributes of his essence and we have neither cause nor any possibility to distinguish between attributes of "unrelatedness' and attributes of "relatedness" or between attributes of self-relation and attributes of relation to the world, or between ontological and economic, transcendent and transitory attributes. Each distinction of this kind – even if only a conceptual distinction – contains not merely no advancement or deepening of our knowledge of God, but works rather to the detriment of it, in that it then becomes almost impossible to hold fast to the fact that it is the essence – and, indeed, the whole essence – of God which in its revelation offers itself to us and thereby opens itself to us. When God gives himself completely to us and thereby becomes known by us as he who is and will be completely for us, then there is nothing more beyond his revelation, even if eternity will not be long enough to exhaust everything that he is for us. But if in his actions he is everything which he actually is for us in his revelation, then he possesses no other attributes at all – neither ontological nor economic – than those which we perceive in his revelation, especially since his essence as love means that in every relationship brought into being through his relation to us, and thus in every attribute, God manifests his whole essence, or, that in every attribute all other attributes are connoted' (*Die christliche Lehre von den Eigenschaften Gottes*, 2nd ed.; Gütersloh, 1917, p. 19f.).

2. The fact that what is to be known about God's being is made known to us from God's being, is based on the fact that God's being for us is event in Jesus Christ. This event is called revelation and as such is God's interpretation of himself.

3. God's being-for-us does not define God's being but certainly God in his being for us interprets his being.

4. Interpretation lives from that which is to be interpreted. As relational being God's being-for-us is the reiteration of God's self-relatedness in his being as Father, as Son and as Holy Spirit.

5. In reiteration that which is to be reiterated lets itself be known. In God's being-for-us God's being-for-himself makes itself known to us as a being which grounds and makes possible God's being-for-us.

6. God's being corresponds to itself
   (a) in the event of God's self-relatedness: as the relation of Father, Son, and Holy Spirit.
   (b) in the event of revelation: as the relation of God's being-for-us to God's being in the event of his self-relatedness.

The correspondence-relation (b) derives its ontological power from the correspondence-relation (a). The correspondence-relation (a) constitutes the correspondence-relation (b).

7. This constituting is itself to be thought of as the power which is proper to the correspondence-relation (a), in which the *hidden* God is the God who *reveals* himself. God's being hidden and God's being revealed is, as relational being, a being in the power of becoming.[159]

[159] If the becoming is comprehended as the ontological place of God's being, then the misunderstanding that God in becoming would become an other, is excluded. 'The one thing that God cannot do is to cease to be God' (*CD* IV/1, p. 40). I should not be surprised when the reader who is not well disposed towards the above, necessarily subtle discussion begins to complain about a way of speaking scarcely intelligible for 'poor theological readers who are used to simplicity' (as, for example, Wolfgang Müller does in a review – noteworthy on account of its brevity – of my book *Paulus und Jesus*, in the journal *Wort und Tat* 18, 1964, Heft 1). Over against this is to be said that I regret my inability to formulate the problem to be treated even more subtly. And so I gladly join with such critics in the confession of the shorter form of the *Shemoneh esreh* (which is current in the school of R. Meir), which runs: 'The needs of thy people are great and their knowledge (understanding) is small.'

It only remains to consider one last reflection. In that we called God's being a being in becoming we understood that God can reveal himself. But that God does what he can, that he has reiterated himself in his revelation, this rests on no necessity. That is much more grace. Yet this grace is not strange to God's being. How otherwise would it be distinguished from necessity? God's grace is rather the reiteration of God's 'Yes' to himself (which constitutes God's being) in relation to something other. In so far as this 'Yes' in relation to something other than God first calls this 'something other' into being, God's gracious 'Yes' sets his being in relationship to the nothing. But in so far as this 'Yes' of grace frees the creation which has been called into being from the threatening which comes through the nothing, God's gracious 'Yes' exposes his being to the nothing. In the last resort, therefore, God's grace signifies God's own self-surrender. But if God's self-surrender is not also God's abandoning of himself, then God's self-relatedness wanted to prove itself precisely in God's relation to the nothing.

God's self-relatedness thus springs from the becoming in which God's being is. The becoming in which God's being is is a becoming out of the word in which God says Yes to himself. But to God's affirmation of himself there corresponds the affirmation of the creature through God. In the affirmation of his creature, as this affirmation becomes event in the incarnation of God, God reiterates his self-relatedness in his relation to the creature, as revealer, as becoming revealed and as being revealed. This Christological relation to the creature is also a becoming in which God's being is. But in that God in Jesus Christ *became* man, he is as creature exposed to perishing. Is God's being in becoming, here, a being unto death?

The witness of the New Testament answers this question with the message of the death and resurrection of Jesus Christ. This message witnesses that there, where God's being-in-becoming was swallowed up in perishing, the perishing was swallowed up in the becoming. Therewith it was settled that God's being *remains* a being in becoming. With his 'Yes' to man God remains in the event of the death of Jesus Christ true to himself as the triune God. In the death of Jesus Christ God's 'Yes', which constitutes all being, exposed itself to the 'No' of the nothing. In the resurrection of Jesus Christ this 'Yes' prevailed over the 'No' of the nothing. And precisely with this victory it was graciously settled why there is being at all, and not rather nothing. For:

> Were he not raised,
> Then the world would have perished;
> But since he is raised
> Then praise we the Father of Jesus Christ.
> Kyrie eleison![160]

[160] In such praise of God, faith confesses that while 'man may deny God, according to the word of reconciliation God does not deny man' (*CD* IV/3, p. 119). And *thus* one will be allowed to say and will have to say that there is – thank *God*! – no being of God in-and-for-itself without man. Only where that is perceived is theology on the way to fulfilling the task set it – so well and pertinently formulated by Gollwitzer – namely: 'to bring the word "God" out of its many meanings and to make its true meaning plain' (*Gottes Offenbarung und unsere Vorstellung von Gott*, Munich, 1964, p. 8).

INDEX OF NAMES